The Life of St. Benedict Joseph Labre

Rev. Giuseppe Loreto Marconi

Translated by
Rev. James Barnard

Sensus Fidelium Press

Contents

Appendix

The Author's Preface, Prefixed To The Italian Edition

Almighty God, who alone does wonderful things, who raises up the needy from the dust, and lifts up the poor from the dunghill, that He may sit with the princes, and hold the throne of glory, has vouchsafed in our days to raise up a poor man, who was born in France, and known by the name of Benedict Joseph Labre, and in proportion to the obscurity of his life, has rendered him so much more illustrious after his death. And, as we piously believe, has put him in possession of that blessed kingdom promised to the poor in spirit; as a proof of which He exerts the power of His right hand, and renews His prodigies.

All of Italy has already been surprised and astonished; and the wonderful works, which are said to be wrought every day not only in Rome, but also in very distant places, are more manifest and more astonishing than his extraordinary virtues, which his most profound humility always made him extremely industrious to conceal. In consequence of such a number of surprising events, which happened immediately after his death, there arose in all people a natural desire to know what kind of man this was, by whom God was pleased to work so many wonders; and what were the qualities and virtues with which he had been adorned. Which, beginning to be rumored about, some officious persons (I know not out of what motive) have set themselves about printing several things concerning him, partly from common report, partly from mere imagination, and some that were even manifestly false. And some others have done the same in some distant places.

It was therefore wisely resolved by the Superiors here in Rome, to forbid the publication of such uncertain and false accounts; and to order that a true and faithful history of his life should be published, which might confute the false reports already spread abroad; and at the same time satisfy the desire which the faithful universally entertain of having a proper account of everything relating to this Servant of God. This charge was consequently committed to me, because I, having been his Confessor, it was imagined I might have a better knowledge of him than any other person. And as I was in duty bound, so I readily consented to undertake it: to which I was also prompted by the esteem and affection which I always entertained for this poor Servant of Jesus Christ, whose life I now publish. The title prefixed to this work is sufficient to show that my design is to give such a clear account of this Servant of God, as may enable my readers to form a sufficient, if not a complete idea of him: in consequence of which I have not spared either labor, diligence, or endeavors to obtain the most accurate intelligence concerning him. So that where I relate any facts that happened at a distance from Rome, I have endeavored by letters, and the help of friends, to procure the most certain vouchers, as the reader will observe in the course of the work: though I have often, for very good reasons, suppressed the names of the persons from whom, and by whose means, I obtained the said intelligence.

I have also had in my possession the authentic documents which have been transmitted to Rome by the Bishop of Boulogne, which he ordered to be collected with the utmost exactness, in the country where this Servant of God was born, and where he resided for several years: amongst which are the depositions of his Father and Mother.

As to those things that have happened in Rome, I have heard the accounts of them from persons of the utmost veracity, who were eyewitnesses of the facts. Nor have I contented myself with having asked them only on one occasion: but I have often and at distant periods of time, interrogated them concerning the things they related; on purpose to see whether the accounts they gave afterwards, agreed with what they had said before. And I have moreover desired them to give me in writing under their own hands, the accounts which they had before given me by word of mouth.

Neither have I relied on the testimony of any person who did not declare himself ready to confirm his assertion on oath in the Process of the Beatification and Canonization of the Servant of God, which is now going on. For which reason I have at proper times inserted the very words in which the attestations of the witnesses are couched; which attestations I now have by me: and likewise a copy of the Verbal Process, formed after his death and before his burial. So that I shall not relate anything but for which I can produce good vouchers. I must also acquaint the benevolent reader that in the many things concerning which I have not had recourse to any other person as a witness; it is because I myself am voucher for them: as I, though unworthy, had the happiness to be his Director: and on that account have had many conversations with him, in which he has given me a most minute account of all the transactions of his life, even from his most tender years. Though, not to tire the reader, I shall not ordinarily in the course of this Life, mention those conversations; but only now and then, when I shall think it more necessary to manifest some glorious thing which happened to him, and which now appears to be verified. But although I have used all possible diligence and endeavors to acquire a true and perfect knowledge of what I relate; yet I may in some things be mistaken, as every man is liable to be in human affairs. For which reason I desire no other credit than that of a historian, and such as may be due to the things which I relate. I hope the reader will excuse the style being plain and common, such as is used by the common people: as what I write is designed to promote the good of all, by proposing to every reader, whether learned or unlearned, the virtuous examples of this Servant of God for his imitation; for which reason I have chosen to relate his virtues, rather than his miracles. And where I have spoken of these, I have done it rather in general words, than given any particular account of them; as I thought it my duty to do so.

Lastly, in confirmation of what I have said at the beginning of this Preface, I think it proper here to mention the words of that worthy Priest Mr. Vincent, Rector of Œuf à S. Pol, who expresses himself in his letter in the following manner: "The life of this man, which, till this present time, did not appear to have anything remarkable in it, and was in a manner totally disregarded; now appears full of interesting and important matter, variegated with an infinite multitude of circumstances, proved by a great multitude of witnesses, and edifying in every one of its parts. And such indeed was the life which he led in all his pilgrimages, and here in Rome itself. Wherefore, dear Reader, I will conclude with what S. Bernard says of S. Malachias. *You have in him something to wonder at, and something to imitate.* Habe in illo quid mireris, habes quid imiteris. This is what I earnestly desire for your good: for the glory of God; and for the exaltation of this His Servant.

The Translator's Preface

Scarcely had the accounts of the wonders wrought by the Almighty, at the Tomb, and by the Intercession, of this His Servant, arrived in England, that everyone was desirous of hearing them: and wished to have them committed to writing. It was, however, judged more prudent to wait, till information concerning the particulars of his extraordinary life could be obtained and reduced into the form of a regular history: which must undoubtedly be more satisfactory to the public, than the publication of unconnected pieces. This has now been done by the Rev. Mr. Joseph Marconi, the Confessor of Benedict, who published his Life in Italian; and an abridgment of it has been made in French, from which this edition is translated.

After what Mr. Marconi has said in his Preface, it is useless for me to add anything more, either concerning the life itself or the care which has been taken to give a true history of this extraordinary man.

This edition consists, first, of a history of the Life of this venerable Servant of God, from his birth until his body was laid in the grave, and which is a faithful translation from the French edition, as anyone may evidently see who is acquainted with both languages. To which I have added an Appendix, wherein I have given an account of several of the extraordinary cures said to have been wrought both at his tomb and in other places, in favor of those who invoked his intercession and desired him to pray for the relief of their respective infirmities, which I have taken partly from the Appendix to the French edition of his life and partly from original letters sent from Rome and other places.

I have already seen in the Gazetteer and the New Daily Advertiser for October 5, 1784, a pretended extract of a letter from an English Gentleman at Boulogne, dated Sept. 27, wherein the writer publishes the fictions of his own brain under the title of Benedict's miracles. I say the fictions of his own brain; because that which he calls by the name of *Miracle*, No. 1, is every word of it an absolute forgery: as nothing like it is mentioned either in the printed account of Benedict's life, or in any letter sent from Rome relating to him. That which he calls *Miracle*, No. 2, has indeed some foundation; but is, according to the common practice of the ridiculers of miracles, misrepresented. Indeed, I do not in the least wonder at this; because, as this real or pretended letter-writer is fully convinced that no miracles were ever wrought in his church: he thinks, the only way to save the credit of his religion, is to ridicule those which God is pleased, even now to work in the Church of Rome.

Those who ridicule miracles may be divided into two different classes. The first consists of those persons, who, being professed Deists and denying all revealed religion, ridicule the miracles of Moses, the prophets, and of Jesus Christ Himself, as well as those of all succeeding ages. The other consists of those who indeed profess themselves Christians and believe the miracles which are recorded in the Holy Scriptures, but at the same time say that miracles have long ago ceased in the Christian Church.

To those of the first class I shall now say nothing, as it is not at present my business to propose the motives of credibility for the conversion of professed infidels. But I think those of the second class should not deny and ridicule miracles, merely because no miracles were wrought in their own church; lest they should hereafter be found to be (as in reality they are) in circumstances exactly similar to those of the Scribes and Pharisees, who shut their eyes against the light that came to enlighten them that sat in darkness, and to guide their feet in the way of peace, and denied and resisted the miracles of Jesus Christ, which He wrought while He was on earth, to convince mankind that He was the promised Messiah, and which if He had not wrought, they would not have sinned in rejecting Him; but which being wrought, they had no excuse for their sin.

What is particularly remarkable in those gentlemen, who ridicule the miracles which God has in all ages continued to work, by the relics and intercession of those who have served Him faithfully on earth, and are now glorified by Him in heaven; is that they tread in the very steps of the Pharisees who rejected Christ, and His doctrine and miracles. When the man who was born blind had received his sight by the miraculous power of our Savior, the Pharisees asked him how he had obtained his sight?[1] He answered, "That man that is called Jesus, made clay, and anointed my eyes, and said to me: "Go to the pool of Siloé, and wash." And I went, I washed, and I see. They then would not believe that he had ever been blind and examined his parents, whether he was their son, and whether he was born blind. Concerning which, when his parents had satisfied them, they still would not acknowledge the miracle. And when on another occasion[2] one was brought unto Him, possessed with a devil, blind, and dumb; and He healed him, so that he both spoke and saw. Although this miracle was wrought in the presence of the Pharisees themselves, yet they would not acknowledge the power to be from God; but said, "This man casteth out devils through Beelzebub, the prince of the devils." In like manner, though miracles be wrought, though they be attested in the most authentic manner, yet those modern Pharisees either deny the facts, attribute the accounts given of them to some underhand juggling, or which is more common, endeavor to get rid of those stubborn proofs of the True Religion by ridicule, when solid arguments fail them.

But, say they, we have very good reason to reject and look upon as impostures, all miracles said to be wrought in the Church of Rome; because all such miracles would tend to prove a false, a superstitious, and idolatrous religion to be the true pure Religion of Jesus Christ. This very thing shows still more how closely these gentlemen tread in the steps of the Pharisees; and the argument which these make use of, is the very same which induced those to reject the miracles of Jesus Christ. They looked upon Him to be an impostor, who had set Himself up for the promised Messiah: an enemy to their law; and the founder of a new religion contrary to the Law of Moses; they had determined to put out of the Synagogue everyone who believed in Him: they looked upon all the miracles that He wrought, as tending to confirm that new, and as they thought, that false religion which He preached and propagated; they likewise accused Him of blasphemy, and took up stones to throw at Him for asserting that He was the Messiah, and that He had existed before Abraham; and moreover declared that He could not be a Prophet, or from God, because He wrought some of His miracles on the Sabbath, which they considered as a profanation of that day. And in a word, the Jewish Pharisees were as fully persuaded that no real miracle could be wrought in confirmation of the Christian Religion which Jesus Christ then preached; as our modern Christian Pharisees are, that no real miracle can be wrought in confirmation of the Religion taught in the Church of Rome. As therefore, on the one hand, the miracles of Christ proved Him to be the promised one, and His doctrine divine; so on the other, that doctrine, which is confirmed by miracles wrought in the name of Christ, must be the doctrine He taught, and is thereby fully vindicated from every aspersion of falsehood or superstition.

It is the misfortune of the Christian Pharisees, as well as it was of the Jewish Pharisees, to begin to examine these subjects at the wrong end. That is, they first lay it down as an undoubted principle, that the Church of Rome is a superstitious and idolatrous Church; and from thence they draw this conclusion: That whatever miracles are said to be wrought in the Church of Rome, cannot be true miracles, but must necessarily be either forgeries or juggles. That is, they make the doctrines the test whereby to judge of the truth of the miracles; instead of making miracles the test whereby to judge of the truth of the doctrines. Though if they would but reflect on what they read in their Bible, they would find that the power of working miracles was given to Moses, to the Prophets, and to the Apostles, in order to convince mankind of the truth of their doctrine, and that they were commissioned by God to teach it. And our Savior Himself appealed to His miracles for the truth of His doctrine, and of His being the promised Messiah. For, says He, "If I had not done among them the works which no man ever did, they would not have had sin; but now they have no excuse for their sin."

But, say they, Antichrist will work a great many lying signs and wonders, insomuch as to deceive, if it were possible, even the very Elect. And how then shall we know which are true, and which are false miracles; but only by the doctrines taught by those who perform those miracles? The words of our Savior are very true: And the consequence they draw from them is also very true in the proper and peculiar sense and signification of the words of our Savior; though not according to that extent to which Protestants want to strain them. Antichrist, spoken of by our Savior, as we learn from St. Paul, is that Man of Sin who will deny Christ, and set himself up in the Temple of God to be worshipped as God, and will do his endeavors to destroy the very name, as well as the public profession of Christianity. And being assisted by infernal power, will do many lying signs and wonders, whereby many will be deceived. But the Elect will avoid that deception, because they will know and be firmly convinced, that according to the promises of God in the Old Testament, and of Jesus Christ in the New, the Church which He established is to last forever even to the end of the world. That it is not to be succeeded by any other religion, as was the case of the Law of Moses. They will moreover remember, that Christ has warned them of the coming of this man of perdition, and of the lying signs and wonders which he will work. And therefore they will conclude, that he who by his proceedings fulfills the prediction of Christ and His Apostles, by his denying

Christ, by endeavoring to destroy the Religion of Christ, and by setting himself up in the temple of God, to be worshipped as God; is that very man of perdition against whom He has warned them. But as this man of perdition is only one single person, and as his proceedings will be so diametrically contrary to the person and religion established by Christ, those who believe Christ to be God blessed forever, cannot avoid knowing Antichrist by these signs: so this is the singular, the only case in which doctrines, once established by miracles, are to be the test whereby Christians are to judge of the signs and wonders of Antichrist.

Moreover, we know not of what kind the lying signs and wonders which will be wrought by Antichrist will be; but this we know, that they will be lying signs and wonders: not real miracles, like those of Moses, the Prophets, of Christ, and the Apostles. But whenever any such miracles as were wrought by Christ and His Apostles, are or shall be wrought by one who believes in Christ, and openly professes his faith: such miracles are always the work of God, done by the finger of God: and are always infallible vouchers of the truth of that religion which he teaches or professes.

Those who profess themselves Christians, and yet deny and ridicule all the miracles which have been properly vouched and attested, thoroughly examined, and solemnly approved as true miracles by the Church of God, would do well to consider what a handle they give to Deists, and other professed infidels, to deny all revealed religion, and to ridicule as impostures, those miracles which are recorded in the very Scriptures themselves. For all the books of the New Testament, and consequently all the miracles therein recorded, are handed down to us only by the testimony of the same Church of God. And consequently, all the certainty we can have that they are books written by the Apostles, and by divine inspiration, depends upon the veracity of the same Church of God. And every Deist and other infidel will very reasonably argue, that if the miracles said to be wrought since the days of the Apostles are false and fictitious, no one can show any reason why those mentioned in the Scripture should not be looked on in the same light: for if it may be supposed, that the Church has forged the accounts of those later miracles said to have been wrought since the days of the Apostles, it may with equal propriety be supposed, that she has forged the accounts of the miracles said to have been wrought by Christ and His Apostles; and likewise everything else contained in the books which relate them.

I will only add, that as Protestants generally pretend, that the miracles wrought in the Church of Rome[3] are only wrought among themselves, when they are not needed; and where a free inquiry into them is not allowed; they have now an opportunity of making, by the means of their Protestant correspondents residing in Rome, all the inquiries which their curiosity, or their incredulity can suggest. But if they think that inquiries by letters are too troublesome or too tedious, and have no objection against taking a short summer's jaunt for their diversion, to Amette, or Hesdigneul near Béthune in French Flanders: they will find hundreds of witnesses to attest so much concerning the former infirm state of Mary Helena Bayard, and her present healthy state; as likewise several witnesses (and among the rest the said Mary Helena Bayard herself) to attest the mode of cure: as will fully satisfy them that her cure was really miraculous. But if they now refuse or neglect to make this enquiry: let them not pretend hereafter, that they have never had an opportunity of enquiring into the truth and reality of such miracles.

Chapter 1

The Birth of the Servant of God; His Infancy and Education

Frace, which is already so famous in the Annals of Religion for the great and holy men it has produced, may now exult in the increase of its glory by having produced in our age an extraordinary man who, during the whole course of his life, being concealed among the common people under the contemptible veil of a poor, mean, and abject life, in the very instant of his death, burst from obscurity; and both by the sudden luster of a multitude of wonders which fame has published through all countries, and by the reputation of an eminent holiness; fixes upon his tomb the admiration of Rome, and the respectful attention of the whole Catholic world.

By these faithful lineaments the reader will immediately know that I allude to the poor servant of Jesus Christ, Benedict Joseph Labre, the relation of whose life, according as the particulars of it may become public, ought to form a tender and lasting impression of religion and piety in the heart of every Christian.

The Diocese of Boulogne upon the Sea was the happy country which gave birth to this illustrious penitent. He was born in the Parish of St. Sulpice of Amettes, on the 26th of March 1748, in the pontificate of Benedict XIV of immortal memory, and in the glorious reign of Louis XV of France.

His father, John Baptist Labre, and his mother, Anna Barbara Grandfire, are both yet living, in decent circumstances. God gave His blessing to their marriage, and sent them fifteen children, of whom Benedict Joseph was the eldest. Their patrimony and their business afforded them sufficient means to give a proper education and establishment to their numerous family.

Touched with a proper sense of gratitude to God for the blessings He had bestowed upon them, they diligently applied themselves to train up their children in innocence and holiness, and to set them an example of a meek and compliant behavior, which still continues to distinguish them among persons of their own rank and condition.

This Servant of God was baptized by his father's brother, Mr. Francis Joseph Labre, formerly vicar and afterward rector of the Parish of Erin, in the Diocese of Boulogne, who was also his godfather and gave him the name of Benedict Joseph. His godmother was Anna Theodora Hazembegue.

Benedict Joseph had the happiness to have this reverend ecclesiastic for his master, who took upon himself the care of his education, and under whose instructions he passed the greatest part of his youth.

He was formed to piety in his infancy, by the instructions and examples of his virtuous parents, who immediately endeavored to unfold the precious buds which grace had shot forth in his soul, and which speedily produced the fruits of an innocent and holy life.

The Servant of God well knew the worth and importance of this first education; he expressed his satisfaction and his gratitude for it, in a letter which he wrote to his parents from Montreuil on the 2nd of October 1769, and he respectfully entreats them to educate his brothers and sisters according to the same plan. "This," says he, "is the means of making them happy in Heaven: for without instruction they cannot be saved. I assure you that you have now done with me: I have cost you a great deal, but be assured that, by the help of God's grace, I shall reap the benefit of all that you have done for me."

A solid judgment, a retentive memory, a quick apprehension even to liveliness, but to a liveliness tempered with a great deal of sweetness and docility; composed the character of Benedict Joseph.

In him the first dawnings of reason appeared to be intermixed and confounded with the first rays of divine grace. His soul immediately opened to, and entertained a tender devotion, which turned his first thoughts towards God. The Holy Ghost, to render him more attentive to his inspirations, gave him, even from that time, a singular love of prayer and retirement. His parents in their depositions, say that[1] they always remarked in him a disregard and contempt of childish amusements.

The Holy Scripture gives this remarkable eulogium of young Tobias[2], that though he was the youngest of all those who composed the Tribe of Naphtali, yet he did no childish actions. And S. Bernard speaking of S. Malachias, gives an account of the first years of his life, in the following words[3]: "His youth seemed intended to render more amiable, and attracting the holy gravity of old men, whom he imitated in his conduct. By his serious and peaceable disposition, his sweet and ready obedience to his superiors, his love of study and of the exercises of young men; it seemed as if the grace of God had utterly extinguished in him all inclination to play and to the amusements of children. And everyone admired in this child of benediction, all the qualities and virtues of men who had attained to years of perfect maturity." And everyone who gave testimony of what passed in the infancy of Benedict Joseph, applied to him the same eulogium.

From the time he was five years of age, he showed a very earnest desire for learning to read and write. This eagerness arose from a holy impatience which he experienced of becoming better acquainted with the rudiments of religion, by acquiring a facility of reading them, and of writing them with his own hand. A sensible joy appeared in his countenance, when having learned to spell, he was able to read distinctly the words of the Lord's Prayer, the Angelical Salutation, and the Apostles' Creed.

The operations of grace ought by no means to be confounded

with what is purely the gift of nature. The moderation, the tranquility, and the sweet and pacific disposition, which constituted the principal part of the character of Benedict Joseph, and which appeared in him from his earliest infancy, were the works of grace, not the effect of constitution.

The particulars of his life furnish a great number of proofs that he was naturally of a lively disposition; but a profound humility, which made him earnestly desire to be disregarded and even despised by men, cast an impenetrable veil over and concealed from the eyes of mankind these natural qualities of his heart and of his mind.

Being a descendant of Adam, he soon perceived that there was in man a law in the flesh, waging war against the law of his mind. And being always obedient to the motions of Divine Grace, every assault of his passions convinced him that the life of a Christian in this world is a continual warfare: and that a Soldier of Jesus Christ must never lay down his Arms, till the moment in which he is to receive his crown. From hence proceeded that courageous resolution, which he formed from his infancy, and which he firmly adhered to, of restraining the first motions of his natural passions and inclinations, and of always corresponding with the grace of God, that in all things he might be guided entirely by the lights and motions of his Divine Spirit.

His Masters, his Parents, and other persons, who had the care of him from his infancy, bear witness that they always observed him to be naturally (as they thought) of a mild, and even bashful temper. And those who have endeavored to study and penetrate into the sentiments and real motives of his conduct, look upon this testimony as proof that in him Grace triumphed over Nature. So that the humility which rendered him mean and contemptible in his own eyes made him endeavor under the external appearance of simplicity, to conceal the violence of his interior conflicts, and the merit of his victories over his natural dispositions.

Chapter 2

The Same Subject Continued: The Employments of the Servant of God in His Infancy

The infancy of those whom God has specially chosen to execute the extraordinary decrees of His Divine Providence is almost always a kind of miniature of what they will be when arrived at years of maturity. And we are furnished with a new proof of this truth in the life of Benedict.

Corresponding with the motions of Divine Grace, which indicated to what kind of life he was called by God, he at five years of age began to execute the resolution of making his soul as much as possible, a most perfect model and copy of our Divine Savior Jesus Christ.

This was one of his common and frequent reflections, that a Christian who sincerely desires to perfectly imitate and become conformable to Jesus Christ, ought to have in some manner three hearts, founded on, proceeding from, and centered in one: that is to say, one for God, another for his neighbor, and the third for himself.

The first, said he, ought to be pure and sincere, always tending to an eminent degree of holiness; continually aspiring to the love of God, with a desire to serve Him, and to submit with patience and resignation to every affliction with which it shall please Him to afflict us during the course of this mortal life.

The second heart, said he, ought to be faithful, generous, and inflamed with charity for our neighbor, always ready to serve him, and particularly employed in sighs and prayers for the conversion of sinners, and for the relief of the faithful departed.

The third, said he, ought to be steady in its first resolutions, austere, mortified, zealous, and courageous, continually offering itself in sacrifice to God. Such ought to be the heart of a Christian, who, being the disciple of a crucified God, will not allow any gratification of his sensual inclinations, but keeps his body in subjection by the wholesome severities of self-denial; and is persuaded that the happiness of the next life will be proportioned to the contempt which in this life he has entertained for this sinful body to which he is chained; and the courage and resolution with which he has kept it nailed to the Cross.

In fine, said he, these three hearts, or affections, ought to be so united as to make only one, which should be amiable to all, a friend of peace, and above all truly humble: for whoever builds upon any other foundation than that of humility, builds upon sand. Such were the great ideas, which from the most tender age this child of Grace entertained concerning the perfection of a Christian life.

In order to form within himself by the help of divine grace, this first Heart, which ought to be dedicated entirely to divine love: he took for the rule of his conduct, a purity of conscience easily to be alarmed and terrified even with the slightest faults; such a horror of sin as made him dread and avoid the slightest occasions of temptation, an exact correspondence with every divine inspiration, and a lively and active faith continually attentive to, and fixed on his divine pattern.

Conformable to his idea of forming a heart inflamed with Charity for his neighbor, he made a resolution of always expressing the real sentiments of his soul, with simplicity, frankness, and candor; of excluding from his thoughts all rash judgments and suspicions; of loving his neighbors with disinterested love; and of offering himself to serve them by every means which his zeal could suggest; but above all, to assist them by his prayers, which was the means most in his power, and which at the same time appeared to him to be the best and most efficacious.

And to form in himself a heart which might be conformable to that of his crucified Savior, he resolved to make it his indispensable practice, to chastise his body and bring it into subjection, by a privation of all sensual satisfactions, by the exercise of continual self-denials and mortifications, and by treating it with a great deal of contempt; that thereby he might prevent any rebellion of the flesh against the law of the Spirit.

Nothing can be more edifying than these maxims which he laid down as the foundation of an Evangelical life; and to which he perceived in himself a particular vocation. His first maxim was to entertain an equal degree of distrust in his own strength, and of confidence in the succors of the grace of God; the second was to apply himself without ceasing to acquire a true knowledge of God, and of himself; the third was, to die to himself, that he might live only, and according to, the life of his crucified Savior; and the fourth, courageously to put on the armor of God, which is prayer, mortification, a renunciation of the world and its dangerous allurements; and above all, interior solitude, and a life of prayer, which is the school of true wisdom, and has always been fruitful in producing holy and evangelical souls.

To declare what were his maxims and his resolutions is just the same thing as to say, what was the continual practice of his life. The testimony given by his parents proves how exactly he observed these maxims even from his most tender years.[1]In proportion, say they, as he advanced in age, he increased also in wisdom both before God and man. "In proportion," say they, "as he advanced in age, he increased also in wisdom both before God and man."

In his infancy, instead of other childish plays, he used to make little oratories, which was a presage of that devotion which, during the whole course of his life, inclined him to look upon as a particular favor the being permitted to serve the priest at the celebration of the

Sacred Mysteries. A practice for which, as his parents testify, he always had a great desire.

A respect for the churches was another of the virtues which was particularly remarkable in his infancy. Being struck with the majesty of those sacred places, and with the sanctity of the venerable mysteries therein celebrated, he never entered into them but with such a degree of reverence as afforded edification to every beholder.

When a soul is free from every earthly affection, and full of God, whom the liveliness of its faith represents as being in a state of immolation upon the altars; when a soul is truly sensible of, and truly grateful for all His favors; where can such a soul experience more celestial sweetness than in the temples and before the holy altars? After the first sketches which we have given of the infancy of Benedict, we ought not to be surprised at what we learn from a multitude of witnesses, as well with regard to his readiness and diligence in assisting at the Divine Service, as with regard to the tender devotion and holy eagerness with which he sought after instruction in the principles of Christianity. The principal occupations, and almost the only delights of this Servant of God in his tender age, were to hear, to read, and meditate on the word of God.

In France, and principally in the country places, on Sundays and festival days, after having assisted at the Evening Office of the Church, it is the custom of the people to spend the rest of the day in different recreations. The compliance and respect which Benedict entertained for the will of his parents and his masters seem to have been the only motives which led him to these public amusements[2]: "but without any relish or inclination for these diversions; on the contrary, he would frequently leave them to go and converse with more aged and serious persons."

There are a great number of children whose giddiness and levity is unconquerable; they fatigue themselves by their natural vivacity, and every day form new inclinations and with the utmost eagerness pursue every object of pleasure which presents itself to their imagination. There are also some others whose indifference for pleasures proceeds from nothing but a mere stupidity of soul, and whose apparent early gravity is nothing but the effect of a melancholic disposition. But the gravity and recollection of young Labre, and his retiring from the ordinary amusements of those of his age, proceeded from a pure and exalted motive. For whenever either obedience or civility rendered it a kind of duty, he would always with a good grace engage in innocent diversions. He was, says his Uncle M. Vincent, "always cheerful in his recreations, and contented with his companions."

If then while he was an infant we find in him none of the defects of infants, if we find in him nothing of that giddiness, levity, impatient desires, no disgust against spiritual things, no repugnance to labor, no love of that liberty and independence which we generally remark in other children; this can be attributed only to God who was pleased to enlighten his budding reason, and incline him to contemn the ordinary imperfections and follies of that age: and to instruct his young soul in the knowledge of the means that were most proper to curb his natural vivacity, and restrain the first sallies of self-love. This can be attributed only to the grace of Jesus Christ, who deigned to make him a model of the most profound humility; in good time gave him to understand, and seriously to reflect on that word which he always addresses to those whom he calls to a state of perfection. "Learn of me, for I am meek and humble of heart."

The young Labre at the same time began to show an early desire and relish for silence and retirement. For the Holy Ghost, who was pleased to choose from a class of men whom our pride and vanity look on with disdain, a striking model of devout and contemplative life: from that time engaged Benedict to follow his vocation, and taught him by a happy experience, in what manner the pleasures which the communication with mankind affords, leave an emptiness in the soul, which has begun to be united to its God by silence and retirement.

Nevertheless, this serious and composed disposition of the Servant of God did not hinder anyone from remarking in him, and even in his countenance, signs of a free and open disposition, and a fund of cheerfulness which was natural to him, which he preserved all his life, and the influence of which everyone perceived who looked upon him with attention.

The age of infancy terminated much sooner in him than in the generality of children. For his love of retirement increased in proportion to his love of reading, and to the facility with which he was able to satisfy that inclination. From that time, recreations seemed to him to be nothing but loss of time. And whenever he engaged in them, it was only in consequence of the obedience which he rendered to the commands of his Superiors.

When he knew how to read, says his Uncle, "he very seldom engaged in play or recreations: for instead of taking these innocent pleasures, he used to retire to read some pious book." And at this time also his Uncle began to take notice of some buds of the virtues of self-denial, and self-contempt, which afterwards grew up, and shone in him in an eminent degree.

Being full of an entire confidence in the paternal care of the Almighty, he was always content: and confined himself to receive only with gratitude what his parents were pleased to give, without asking anything, even of those things that were necessary for his subsistence. During the whole course of his life he never departed from this abdication of all earthly things which he had resolved on and practiced from his tender age. But this, which in his infancy was in him a kind of Novitiate to that state of evangelical poverty which he practiced with so much rigor during the rest of his life: was at that time looked upon only as an effect of natural bashfulness.

Chapter 3

His First Studies

The desire which he showed to learn to read and write, determined his parents to send him, when five years old, to the Schools of Auteuil, where he had for his first master M. D'Hannoch, Vicar of that Parish, who then kept those Schools, and was afterwards made Rector of the Parish of Bouvard. He remained under his care till he was between seven and eight years old.

When we make the holy will of God the motive and end of all our actions, then each one of our obligations appears to us to be indispensable: and our zeal every day furnishes us both with time and ability to fulfill those obligations with regularity and diligence. If Benedict was a model of religion and piety to the other children with whom he was educated; he set them an equal and edifying example of docility and alacrity in the discharge of the duties proper to persons of his age.

The letter of M. D'Hannoch is a moving proof of the impression which the sight of the budding virtues of this boy's young disciple left in his soul. "I always knew him," says he in one of his letters, "to be a child of an admirable good disposition, and of a singular and exemplary diligence in discharging the duties corresponding to his age, and endowed with every good quality which I could wish to find in a child; and which rendered his memory so dear to me, that for the space of about eight and twenty years since he left me I never let slip any opportunity of enquiring after him; so much did I expect that some good would attend him."

To this is added the declaration of Francis Joseph Forgeois, who says[1], "that he remarked in this child, that he distinguished himself from all the others of his age, by his modesty, his piety, his docility, his meekness, his tranquility, and his eagerness to learn to read, and to learn the first principles of religion." And Bartholomew Francis de la Rue, another of his masters declares, that "he remarked in him a great deal of piety, docility, meekness, and complaisance for his master; that he never had occasion to be afraid of his master; as being sensible of his having never given him occasion of offence. He moreover declares that he himself was so well satisfied with the conduct of Benedict, that he does not remember, he ever said or did anything that might grieve him."

God has been pleased that the education of Benedict in the first years of his life should be committed to several masters successively in order that by that means he might multiply witnesses of the virtues and extraordinary graces with which he was favored in his infancy. He, in a particular manner, possessed all the virtues suitable to that age: a scrupulous diligence in the discharge of his duties, love of study, respect for his parents, docility and obedience to his masters, and civility to all. But what appeared to be far beyond the capacity of a child, and which nevertheless was the singular character of Benedict, was even at that time a sensible love of retirement and recollection, a remarkable disengagement of his heart from all affection to earthly things, a reigning inclination for piety and, to say all in one word, an anticipated knowledge of that true Christianity which does everything for the love of God; which tends continually towards God, and which in all things endeavors to imitate the poverty and humility of its crucified Savior.

Let us not by any means pretend to measure the wisdom of God by the diminutive scale of the human understanding. God is wonderful in all His Saints. His Providence shines upon His Church in every age with great luster, and in such a manner as renders it more and more visible. In all probability, the reason why God imparted to Benedict while he was yet an infant such extraordinary graces was that by new examples capable of arousing our drowsy faith, He might convince us that His Church, which is always holy, will never cease to have saints of every age, as well as it has saints in every state and condition of life.

Chapter 4

An Account of the Youth of Benedict. His Conduct Under the Direction of His Uncle: He Makes His First Communion

St. Bernard by these remarkable words describes the transition of St. Malachias from a state of infancy to that of youth.

"The youth of St. Malachias was entirely of a piece with his infancy. He preserved the same purity, the same simplicity, the same innocence of morals. The only difference that could be observed in him in those two different stages of his life was, that in his youth he entertained a still greater desire to grow in wisdom and in grace both with God and man: in such manner that besides the common obligations incumbent on him, he took upon himself certain particular devotions and observances; and by this means raised himself to a degree of virtue and holiness to which it was difficult for others to attain."[1]

We may observe a striking likeness between this eulogium which St. Bernard gives of the adolescence of St. Malachias, and the expressions which the parents of Benedict made use of in giving an account of the conduct of their son, from his infancy till he was about twelve years old, which was the time when he left his father's house, and was put under the care of his uncle the Reverend Rector of Erin.

We may see in this happy resemblance between these two characters, and with a satisfaction which is well able to animate our faith, that it is always the same Divine Spirit who makes saints: and that though the fruits of His graces may be different, according to the difference of the ages and states of the persons to whom he imparts them; yet that the source, the foundation, and the substance of the sanctity from whence these fruits proceed, is the same in every age, and in every state: and that by a particular disposition of His Divine Providence, it sometimes happens that children called in their infancy and at the first hour to a life of holiness, and who persevere faithful to their vocation, may be proposed as models to those persons who seem not to hear till the last hours of their life that voice of God which never ceases to call them to a life of holiness.

This conclusion naturally follows from the idea formed in our minds, by the multitude of testimonies of the conduct of Benedict in the course of his infancy and of his youth. "His parents in particular declare, that during the time he continued under their care, he gave them constant proofs of a sincere piety; by his assisting at the Divine Offices and instructions with a degree of attention and reverence truly edifying; of wisdom and prudence, in never saying or doing anything unbecoming; of obedience, by always doing what he was ordered, with cheerfulness and alacrity; of peacefulness, in always behaving towards his father, his mother, his brothers, and sisters in such a manner, as never to give them any occasion of uneasiness or offence; and of a wonderful patience, by bearing the weaknesses and imperfections of his father, his mother, his brothers, his sisters, and those of his age; always maintaining a serene and cheerful counte-nance notwithstanding whatever they said or did to him; and this to such a degree, as to make those who had been culpable, ashamed of their proceedings. A disposition (added his parents) which rendered this child most dear and amiable to them, as he likewise was to everyone who knew him."

The parents of young Labre, being charmed with the good quali-ties of his heart and of his soul, thought that they ought to concur with the designs of God concerning him, by procuring for him, jointly with the knowledge of the Latin tongue, an education superior to that which he would be able to obtain while he should continue in his father's house.

M. Labre, who was both his uncle and his godfather, received from the hands of his parents this young plant, who had already afforded such promising hopes to all those who had had him under their care, and had given him the first cultivation. Benedict during his whole life looked upon it as a singular favor of Divine Providence, that in the most critical age of youth he had been committed to the care and affection of this worthy ecclesiastic, in whom he all at once found a preceptor, a spiritual director, a friend, and a pattern for his initiation.

The Servant of God, being then in the twelfth year of his age, his virtuous uncle thought he ought to begin his course of education by disposing him to make his first Communion; and therefore gave him notice to prepare himself for it.

At this news, his soul was filled with sentiments of joy, of love, of humility, and of a holy fear. These words of the Apostle, *"Let a man prove himself, and so let him eat of that heavenly bread"*, were the most common subject of his thoughts. He had for a long time sighed after this happiness, for which by a long practice of meditation he had acquired the greatest esteem. Before the approach of this happy day, he used his utmost endeavors to cleanse and purify his soul by a general confession. And this was the first out of five or six general confessions which he made in the course of his life.

The method which he took to prepare himself for the Sacrament of Penance is so edifying that it will without doubt be both agreeable and useful to give a particular account of it.

The venerable Benedict, being persuaded that without the grace of God we can do nothing, not even discover our own faults so as to view them in that light in which we ought to consider them, first implored the light of the Holy Ghost, and besought Him not only to bring to his remembrance his sins with all their different circumstances, but likewise to discover to him the true state of his soul, his bias, and inclinations.

After this he seriously examined into the state of his conscience, proceeding according to the order of the Commandments, and to the virtues corresponding to each Commandment; therewith examining and comparing his life and all his actions, from the time he had made his last Confession.

When he examined his conscience for a General Confession, he divided his life into as many spaces of time as he had made general confessions after his first Communion: and then began with the last epoch, and went back in regular order from that to the first.

In the course of this examination he took special care not to make himself the judge of his own actions; this he considered as the province and privilege of the Minister of Jesus Christ. And therefore, that he might not transgress his own bounds, he explained what temptations he had experienced, and how he had behaved under them; as likewise what special graces he had received from Almighty God, and gave a particular account of in what manner he had corresponded with them.

The examination of his conscience being finished, he again had recourse to humble and fervent prayer to obtain of God a true contrition of heart, and endeavored to excite this contrition in his soul, by a serious consideration of all the motives which Faith suggests as leading to it. Above all he endeavored to excite in his soul a sorrow for sin founded on those motives which render it perfect contrition, by considering sin as an ingratitude committed against God, a disobedience to His law, and an outrage offered to His infinite and essential sanctity. And in his accusation of himself he preserved order, clearness, precision, humility, and sincerity, to an admirable degree.

After this he listened to the words of his Confessor with very great respect, submitting his own private opinions to his decisions, being docile to his instructions, and venerating his word as oracles sent from heaven.

Before receiving the Absolution he bowed himself down; and, for some time humbling himself in the presence of Almighty God, renewed his sorrow for his sins, and endeavored to excite in his soul most lively acts of contrition; after which he modestly raised his head to give his Confessor to understand that he was now ready to receive absolution.

He was persuaded in his own mind, and frequently repeated to others this idea, which he said he learnt from S. Teresa, that a multitude of Christians plunge themselves into eternal miseries by making sacrilegious confessions. He distinguished the sinners who went to confession, into three classes: the perfect penitents, the imperfect penitents, and the false penitents; who appeared to him, as forming three processions of people, who in departing from the sacred tribunal of penance, took each a different road.

The first class, which consisted of but very few, was composed of true penitents: these were they who, having probed the wounds of their souls to the bottom, had manifested them with sincerity and without disguise; had entertained a sincere sorrow for them; had bewailed them with truly penitential tears; and without having neglected any of the conditions necessary for a good confession, had afterwards used their utmost efforts to appease the divine justice, by their fasts, their prayers, their alms, and other mortifications, and exercises of piety superadded to the penitential works enjoined them by the ministers of God; and had endeavored, by faithfully performing the conditions required for the gaining of indulgences, to supply what was still wanting in them to fulfill all justice. The Servant of God looked upon these holy penitents as being clothed with a white and luminous robe: who in the moment of their death are carried to heaven, and enter in triumph into the eternal Tabernacles of the living God.

The second class, still very few, yet more numerous than the former, was composed of imperfect penitents, who had their garments tinged with a red color. These were they who had indeed faithfully complied with the conditions essentially necessary for a good confession, and had not rendered the grace of penance useless.

But relying too much on the pardon they had obtained, they had afterwards shown but very little zeal in performing the penitential works prescribed to them by their confessor: and had neglected to have recourse to the Indulgences, which their tender and compassionate mother the Church offers to its penitent and reconciled children, to put them in the way of supplying their own insufficiency of satisfying the divine justice for their sins. Heaven, said he, remains shut against their desires of entering: and they are pushed back towards purgatory to complete that satisfaction, which the Divine Justice demands, and to be entirely purified from everything which has defiled their souls.

The false penitents, who composed the third class, and which was far more numerous than the two former, appeared to him as clothed with dirty and filthy garments: These were they who, either by haste and extraordinary negligence in the examination of their conscience, by being destitute of true contrition or a firm resolution of amendment, by want of sincerity in the acknowledgment of their sins, or by being overcome by a wretched fear or shame, willfully concealed any part of their sins; and by that means defiled their souls with the very waters of that sacred bath which was intended to restore them to their original purity: these appeared to him as sacrilegious hypocrites, who go to hell by the very road which ought, and was intended to lead them to heaven.

These thoughts strongly imprinted in the mind of Benedict a dread and horror of sin. And they contributed to preserve and defend his innocence against temptations, and to render beneficial to him the use of the Sacraments, to which he had recourse to be purified from his sins.

A general confession made according to the method of Benedict is undoubtedly an excellent preparation for the first communion. To which preparation he also added Meditation, Prayer, and some particular Acts of Mortification.

We know says St. Thomas[2], what effects the Bread which came down from Heaven produces, when it is received into a soul well prepared for it. As it is the bread of angels, it makes us pure like them; as it is the blood of God, it in some manner transforms us into God; as it is the tree of life, planted in the hearts of the faithful, it fails not immediately to produce both the flowers which exhale the good odor of true disciples of Jesus Christ, and the plentiful fruits of every Christian virtue.

Those which the grace of his first Communion produced in this servant of God, immediately manifested themselves by a sensible increase of his fervor and piety, and by a more close and perfect union with God; for from this moment he turned all his thoughts and affections towards heaven, continually endeavoring to make his soul a lively model of Jesus Christ, and continually aspiring to such a degree of perfection, that he might say with the Apostle, *I live, or rather it is not I, but Christ who liveth in me.* But his inclination to works of penance and mortification was still more sensible; for from that time, he began to observe all the fast days appointed by the Church with scrupulous exactness; and such was his temperance and niceness in this point, that he would rather tread under his feet the most delicious fruits of his uncle's garden, than offer to taste any of them, which were most capable of alluring him.

He entertained a still more ardent love for his neighbor, for they now began to take notice that he abridged himself of his necessary sustenance, that he might secretly convey to a poor woman that food which was given to him for his own nourishment, and, in this manner by one and the same act, practiced the two Christian virtues of Penance and Almsgiving.

He had also a still more evident love of solitude and retirement: for from this time he began to entertain a total disregard for the world, and all his thoughts and conversation turned towards Heaven. From this time his only delight was to "remain either at the foot of the Altars, or in a little summer house at a distance from his Uncle's dwelling house, and where he was almost continually occupied in reading books of Piety."

Chapter 5

Sentiments of Esteem Which the Uncle, and the School-Fellows of the Servant of God, Entertained for Him

I t commonly happens that a virtuous man gains an ascendant, and a certain kind of natural authority over those with whom he lives, which procures him both their esteem and respect; and which almost always tends to promote piety and virtue among them.

After the description we have already given of the qualities and virtues of this Servant of God, we ought not to be astonished at any of those things that are reported of him, at the impression which his conduct made on the hearts of those who were eyewitnesses of his actions, or at the sentiments and marks of friendship, esteem, and respect which they showed him.

"The children, says Mr. Emadon, Rector of Erin, paid to him at least as great respect as they did to their master on account of his piety." This testimony agrees with that which is given by M. Clement, who says, "that the children observed something in him which inspired them with more respect for him, than the presence of even their Master himself produced."[1] This is likewise attested by many of his former schoolfellows, when they were separately interrogated, in what manner he used to conduct himself in his youth; and whose depositions are contained in the letter of the Reverend Rector of Erin. He says, "They (Joseph Bissell, James Le Gay, and James Louis Thuilliers) have all declared, and assured me, that they always observed him to be very prudent and exemplary in his conduct; that he severely reprimanded them when he saw them do, or heard them speak anything improper, or contrary to the commandments of God; that he was very pious, modest, and devout in the Church; that he constantly assisted at all the divine offices, without ever moving himself; that he always applied himself diligently to read good books; that instead of eating the food that was given to him, he would frequently give it to some poor person out of the window; that when he went to take a walk or other recreation with his uncle the Rector, he carried with him some books of piety, and read them as he walked along; and in a word, that all the time he lived in the parish of Erin, they never saw him do, or heard him speak anything that was any way improper, or contrary to good manners."

Next to the sweetness which flows into the soul of a pious Christian by conversing with God in prayer, it can experience none greater than that of hearing God speak to it by the means of good books; in which employment the servant of God employed every moment of time he could find otherwise vacant. Among the books belonging to his uncle, he found the Sermons of Père le Jeune the Oratorian, who is also and more commonly known by the name of Père l'Aveugle.

The force of his reasoning, founded entirely on the evidence of good sense, the bewitching smoothness of his kind of florid style, the simplicity, and if I may so call it, the popularity of his expressions, would naturally produce in a soul an imagination disposed like that of Benedict, a certain kind of interested pleasure, flowing from a conformity of sentiment; and which in effect it did produce in him. For which reason he made the Sermons of this preacher his favorite books: he had them continually in his hands, and a great and happy memory preserved during his whole life, the deposited truths of Christian morality, which the frequent reading of these Sermons had deeply imprinted in his soul.

Fear and love are the two springs which act most powerfully upon the human heart. And Père le Jeune makes use of these with a great deal of force and pathetic sensibility, particularly in his two sermons, on Hell, and on the small number of the Elect. These sermons made a very deep impression in the soul of this pious young man; and the more so, as he read them at a time when he began seriously to think on choosing a state of life, and this made him redouble his fervor in his prayers, and beg of God to direct him by His grace to choose that, to which His Divine Providence should be pleased to call him.

The pious young man was now near entering into the fifteenth year of his age. And a delicate and timorous conscience, a courageous heart, and a generous soul, trained up from his infancy in the purest and most solid maxims of Piety and Religion, would naturally incline him to embrace a state, which might furnish his ardent spirit with the means which were most likely to raise him to the utmost pitch of human perfection. His inclination to solitude, his retirement and separation from the world, his love of prayer, and of the exercises of piety, which the frequent participation of the Holy Sacraments daily more and more augmented in him; immediately turned his thoughts towards a religious state of life. And the signs of his vocation to this state appeared more certain, inasmuch as for several years, he had exercised himself in the constant practice of poverty, humility, and penance.

Being resolved to choose among the different religious houses, one in which his inclination for the practice of these three virtues might more easily be satisfied; he immediately pitched upon the Abbey of La Trappe, which is rendered famous by having embraced the original rule, and spirit of the Order of St. Bernard, and in which that spirit is with great edification kept up till this very day. After having again by humble and fervent prayer endeavored to know what was the will of God in his regard, and supplicated his divine direction; he made known his desire and intention to his Uncle.

This virtuous ecclesiastic advised him to open the matter to his father and mother. A pious young man will always be respectful, tender, and submissive to his parents. Benedict was the eldest of a numerous family, and his parents had always looked upon him as the child who was to be their principal comfort, and support in their old age. And as he was to inherit a decent patrimony, they entertained thoughts of, and began to look round to see how they might fix him in a happy and peaceful state; but they were afflicted at hearing this their son's resolution. The tenderness of his mother was shocked, particularly at his mentioning the Abbey of la Trappe. They opposed to his desires such a resistance, that his most earnest solicitations were not able to conquer. The humble young man considered their refusal, as one of the trials which Divine Providence was pleased to make of his virtue. His ready obedience forbade every murmur; he returned to his Uncle to put himself again under his direction, and resolved by redoubling his fervor, to endeavor to obtain of God, that he would one day vouchsafe to accept of the sacrifice and dedication of himself, (which he wished to make) to his Divine Service.

Chapter 6

The Servant of God Returns to the Parish of Erin Where He Remains Till the Year 1766

It sometimes happens that disappointments and contradictions weaken a man's resolutions, and cast him into despondency. But that which Benedict experienced by his parents refusing their consent to his going to the Abbey of la Trappe; on the contrary contributed to redouble his fervor, and inspire him with a greater attachment to his duties, a greater love for prayer and for the reading of good books, a greater circumspection in his words, greater reserve in his conduct, greater simplicity in his manners, greater separation from worldly pleasures, and a greater desire of uniting his soul more closely to God by a frequent participation of the Holy Sacraments.

His uncle's house was to him a kind of monastery; where, as much as his situation would allow, he observed a religious poverty, the silence of a cloister, and all the regularity of a religious community. His submission and ready obedience to the will of his uncle, was like that of a religious man to his superior. Being already accustomed to the austerities of a penitential life, he rigorously observed all the fast days commanded by the Church, although, by his not having yet attained to twenty-one years of age, he was exempt from the law of fasting. Such was the conduct of this servant of God for the space of two years and a half, which he spent at Erin: whose virtues are still fresh in the minds, highly esteemed, and frequently spoken of by the inhabitants of that place; the greatest part of whom had been eyewitnesses of his conduct. And the proofs he afforded them of his charity for them, will for a long time render them grateful to his memory.

A cruel epidemic disorder desolated that parish; so that every house was full of persons attacked with it; insomuch, that there was scarcely any person who was able to supply the wants of the sick, or to attend and serve them. These and such like misfortunes to which human nature is subject almost always furnish Religion with matter of triumph; because they always afford a true Christian occasions of exercising his virtues; for he scarcely knows how valuable his life is, but only at the time when he has an opportunity of making a sacrifice of it to God, by serving his brethren.

The virtuous uncle on this occasion showed his zeal and love for his parishioners to be boundless; and the charity of this pious young man inspired him with courage and resolution to brave every danger. To neither uncle nor nephew did the night afford any rest, after the fatigue of the day; but each one, without any relaxation, went hither and thither to afford relief, wherever danger called them; so that there was no one sick person in the whole parish, who was not visited, served, comforted, and assisted.

In country places, the cattle constitute a great part of the fortune of the poor farmers, insomuch that to lose their cattle is to them an evil almost as great as to lose their own lives. Benedict knew this, and therefore he endeavored to render them all the service that was in his power by dividing his labors, partly in taking care of the poor sick persons, and partly in taking care of the cattle that belonged to them.

While his uncle, wholly employed in the exercise of his pastoral office, exposed his life in visiting and comforting the sick, and stripped himself of all that he was worth, to afford relief to his poor parishioners; this charitable young man performed for them the most abject and laborious services. He took care of their cattle, cleaned their stalls; and he, who by the life he had lived with his uncle, and whose education seems to have forbidden him to be employed in menial labors; might be frequently seen running sometimes to the gardens, sometimes to the fields, and returning again loaded with greens, grass, and provender for the cattle and other animals, the care of which he had taken upon himself, and which he distributed to them with his own hands.

So great charity is never exercised without meeting with a proper reward. God, who keeps an account of every cup of cold water given in alms for His sake, without doubt will never forget it: but how different are the thoughts of God, and how much more exalted, than the thoughts of man! The world sometimes gives wealth or titles of honor as the reward of past services; but God frequently sends to His friends new crosses to endure, as the recompense of what they have already done or suffered for His sake. And what is this but the fulfilling of those words of our Savior: *Woe be to them who have received their consolation here,* by which our infinitely wise, and good God gives us to understand that He does not confound the time of combat, with the time of triumph, and of receiving the reward of our victories: but that the most precious recompense for past services which a Christian ought to desire, so long as he shall continue in this life, is that of new occasions of serving, and fulfilling the will of God here, and thereby meriting a more glorious crown hereafter.

It was in this manner that God was pleased to deal with this His servant. The epidemic disorder after a time ceased: but the excess of fatigue had totally exhausted the strength of the worthy Rector of Erin. A fit of sickness, which was the consequence of it, in a few days carried him out of this world, to the great grief of the inhabitants of the parish, who for a long time regretted the loss of their worthy pastor.

What a stroke this was for Benedict, and in what a situation was he left! God had deprived him of a master, a patron, a second father. In his house he found a retreat, which in a great measure alleviated the regret he experienced at finding the monasteries shut against him, by his parents refusing their consent. But the death of his uncle left him almost without support, and seemed to be a presage of new obstacles to the following his vocation. The Servant of God saw the whole extent of his loss: nevertheless, his courage increased with his confidence in God; and the Holy Ghost, speaking interiorly to his soul, gave him to understand that a Christian is never stronger than when he has no reliance but on God alone.

Chapter 7

He Returns Again to His Parents, and Again Endeavors To Obtain Their Consent for Him To Go to La Trappe

The idea and representation of his uncle in the agonies of death was deeply and lastingly imprinted in the mind of this Servant of God, and was in a manner continually before his eyes. It is in this school of the contemplation of death that true Christians are formed to virtue. That important moment discovers the true value of Time and Eternity. For to a wise man who seeks truth with sincerity of heart, and who, upon the tomb of a person who was once dear to him, reads with attention the fragility of man's life and the vanity of the world; God immediately becomes the only object of his desires. These kinds of reflections contributed to awaken in Benedict the thoughts of retirement, and the desire of solitude, that he might have nothing to do but to labor for the salvation of his soul. His humility inclined him to believe that the true obstacle to the success of his hopes and endeavors was his own unworthiness; and for this reason, he used all possible means to render Almighty God propitious to him. He increased the number of his prayers and redoubled his fervor in his devotions. And by the practice of works of penance and particular mortifications, he laid deep the foundation of that life of poverty, austerity, and self-denial, which he afterwards carried to so great a degree of perfection.

It was at this time that he made his second general confession, in order to prepare himself to lead a life more holy, more united to God, and more worthy of being admitted into a religious state, which was the constant object of his wishes.

The Servant of God, being now again returned to his parents after the death of the venerable Rector of Erin, took this occasion to solicit their consent for him to enter into a religious house; and that they would give him leave to go to the Abbey of La Trappe. But he now met with a second repulse, still stronger than that which he had experienced before; particularly from his mother, who was encouraged in her refusal, by the concurrent opposition which the whole family made to his proposal.

But being now eighteen years old, he thought that he might show more firmness and resolution, without in any way deviating from the respect due to his parents. He forcibly urged upon them the necessity of following his vocation and showed them that the reasons which shocked their tenderness, and engaged them to endeavor to turn his thoughts from the resolution he had taken of choosing to go to La Trappe, ought on the contrary to encourage them: because, said he, a constant inclination to a close retirement and to the exercises of the holy austerities of a penitential life, is the most certain sign of a vocation to a Religious state.

The parents of Benedict, having always been very religious, apprehended that by longer resisting the desires of their son, they might probably be found to have resisted what was the will of God. The Servant of God, in consequence of this idea, at length obtained their consent and their benediction. He accordingly left them, and the fatigue of a long journey did nothing but augment his zeal, and the fires of living a poor and mortified life.

What a multitude of sentiments of joy presented themselves to the soul of the Servant of God as soon as he arrived within sight of the Abbey of La Trappe! He now thought himself secure of the object of his wishes: but he here found a new trial of his virtue, where he hoped to have found a place of rest and repose. This Abbey had lately lost a great number of its members; and in order to adapt the ability of its subjects to the severity of its rules, the Superiors had judged it prudent not to admit any persons as new members, but those whose natural constitution was already absolutely formed, and capable of observing the severities of its rule. Benedict arrived a short time after this new regulation had been made. And it was not judged proper to dispense with this rule, so soon after making it, in order to admit him to a trial; and therefore he could not obtain admittance.

The regret which he experienced in consequence of this refusal cannot be expressed. He was struck with a lively and pungent grief; but he bore it with the patience and resignation becoming a true Christian. But as the permission which he had obtained from his parents particularly regarded his going to the Abbey of La Trappe, into which he could not then be received, he immediately returned again to his father's house, to wait with submission to the decrees of Divine Providence, for a more favorable time to put his project into execution.

One of his uncles, who was then Vicar of the Parish of Couteville and Rector of the Schools therein established, was desired to continue his education and perfect him in the knowledge of the Latin tongue. He here found in M. Vincent, all that he had lost by the death of the worthy Rector of Erin. The testimony which the Right Rev. Bishop of Boulogne gives of the virtues of M. Vincent, affords us an opinion of him far greater than every other eulogium.[1] This worthy Ecclesiastic always looked upon his nephew as a model of virtue. He immediately loved him with as much affection as if he were his own son. And Benedict was not behindhand with him but afforded every motive of consolation to his uncle, by his docility and endeavors to profit by his instructions, and his example. The account which M. Vincent himself gives of his pupil, excuses our giving any other particular account of his conduct. It is sufficient to transcribe a part of the affidavit made by this virtuous priest, who is now actually rector of the Parish of La Pelle.

"Benedict Joseph," says he, "rendered himself amiable from his most tender years, on account of his great mildness, of which he has on many occasions given signal proofs at Coutteville, amongst some students whom I then taught. There was one, a very turbulent youth, who knowing him to be of a peaceful disposition, used to make it his diversion to thwart and mortify him: but he never resisted him either by words or actions. He has exercised his patience so far, as that, rather than to resist, or make any complaints against him, he has suffered himself to be very much annoyed with the cold in winter. I have observed in Benedict, a great deal of piety, and inclination to read good books. The works of Père L'Aveugle have given him this inclination, and this ardent desire of leading a penitential life: he has read them several times: and as he had a sound judgment, and a good memory, he has imprinted in his soul, the truths which he took notice of in these books." Father Le Jeune had rendered himself famous by the missions which occupied his zeal during almost the whole course of his life. The esteem which Benedict entertained for his works would naturally excite in his soul a love for those priests who dedicated themselves to this function, which is as laborious as it is respectable. Some missionaries having come into the Diocese of Boulogne, to begin their preaching at Bocaval, Brias, Zoillecourt, and Recquignies, the pious youth followed them in these different parishes and thought of nothing but the salvation of his soul. Beholding the zeal which these fathers (who were of the congregation of the Mission established by St. Vincent de Paul) demonstrated in endeavoring to convert sinners from their evil ways and bring them to a life of virtue and holiness, he applied to Mr. Chomault, who was one of that congregation, and at that time superior of the Seminary of Boulogne, and besought him to hear his general confession, which was the third that he made in the course of his life.

Benedict, who every day sighed after solitude and a place of retirement, was cut to the heart to find his hopes so long delayed.

Finding that his being under the proper age rendered him incapable of being admitted into La Trappe, he thought that he should not meet with so many obstacles if he solicited that favor at some Convent of Carthusians. This he communicated to his Director: who approved of his design; and the pious youth returned to Amette to acquaint his parents with it, and to ask their consent to put it in execution.

Chapter 8

The Servant of God Meets With New Obstacles Again; His Entering Into a Religious State, Both From His Parents and From the Carthusians of Longuenesse and Montreuil

The parents of Benedict, having consented to his following his inclination of embracing a religious state in the Abbey of La Trappe, he had good reason to hope they would not oppose his inclination of entering into another order whose rules were less severe. But in this, he was mistaken, for he found his parents opposed his entrance into a convent of Carthusians no less than they had before opposed his going to La Trappe. They did not fail to represent to him the temporal advantages which he abandoned by such a resolution, the uncertainty of success in his undertaking, the rashness of embracing a state of life which he might not be able to go through, and the utility that he might be of to his family in assisting his parents in the education of his brothers and sisters, and what ought still more to touch him, to the heart, the love of his parents, and the assistance and support which he might thereafter be able to afford them, in case they should by any unforeseen misfortunes be reduced to distress, and every other motive which could show how afflicting to them, would be the separation and sacrifice which he wanted to make of himself to God.

But the aversion which he entertained against the world, the desire of renouncing all things for the sake of God, and that he might live only for His sake, had taken so deep a root in the heart of the servant of God, as not to suffer him to be swayed by worldly or human motives, or to suffer his resolution to be overcome by mere appearances of good, or possibilities of things which were not likely to happen in effect.

At the same time, he met with another obstacle which he before never thought of, and which a second time rendered useless the consent which he had obtained of his parents. For when he went to the Convent of Carthusians at Montreuil, the Prior received him with good nature and affability, spoke to him with cordiality, and gave proofs of his esteem and affection for him; but finished his conversation by objecting to his youth, and by telling him that such was the custom of the house that he could not be admitted until he had studied Philosophy at least for the space of one year, and likewise had learned the Gregorian music called Plain Song. But to comfort him, he added, that as soon as ever he was qualified in those two things, he would receive him with pleasure. Benedict expressed his gratitude for this obliging promise made to him by the Prior, and left Montreuil with intent to return to his parents, but he was informed that the Convent of the Carthusians at Longueness was a house wherein he might in all likelihood be received with greater facility. The Servant of God, in consequence of this information, went to Longueness, and the success which he there met with answered his wishes. The Prior gave him a favorable reception, and admitted him to the exercises of the noviceship.

This epoch of the life of the Servant of God, for those souls whom God calls to a state of extraordinary perfection, is a source of great instruction: it was one of the hardest trials he ever experienced; for corporal austerities are nothing when compared to the anguish of the soul. This solitude which had been the object he had so long sighed after, into which he at once rushed with so much ardor and so much joy, this solitude which he had looked upon as a true land of promise, he soon found to be a land of trouble and affliction, a dry and barren desert.

The masters of an internal and spiritual life know, and they only can well describe that state of obscurity, and sometimes of terrors and anguish, by which God frequently conducts those souls which He destines to attain to a high degree of perfection. This is one of the means which His Divine Providence makes use of, to lay in chosen souls the deep foundations of humility, to make them die to themselves, to divest themselves of all confidence in themselves or others, that He may afterwards attach them closely to Himself by the means of contemplation and love.

The soul which entertains an ardent love, tends always to a union with the object of its love: and it is by the means of contemplation, that love conducts the soul to a union with its beloved object.

The first grace which moves the souls of Christians called to a state of perfection, is a ray of divine light which reveals to them the knowledge of God, and the knowledge of themselves. Employed in the contemplation of these two things, the soul is soon convinced, that God is the being of beings, and the creature a mere nothing: it sees on one hand the immensity of God's greatness, and on the other the abyss of its own wretchedness; an immense sanctity, and an abyss of sin: an immense love, and an abyss of ingratitude.

It is in this manner that the Soul compares what is finite, with what is infinite; the enormity of sin, with the idea which it forms of the infinite holiness of God; the punishment of the sinner, with the infinite justice of God; the ingratitude, or little love which men entertain in their hearts for God, with the infinite charity of God for men; the negligent manner in which they ordinarily perform their duties to their Creator, with the perfection with which His Law requires they should be performed; the severe account which they must one day render of their actions, with the infinite number of the graces and favors they have received from God; and the weakness and insufficiency of their repentance with the multitude of their offenses and imperfections.

But the eye of the Soul, which is the understanding, cannot remain long fixed on the contemplation of this double abyss of the greatness of God, and the wretchedness of man; it cannot embrace at once the infinite distance there is between God and the sinner, and bring both these objects into one point of view, without being immediately overwhelmed with anguish and confusion. Struck with astonishment at the contemplation of the divine perfections, and its own imperfections, the Soul perceives nothing in itself but spots, stains, filthiness, coldness, ingratitude, and weakness. God at that time seems to withdraw Himself from the Soul, and permits that it should be for a time given up to fears and terrors.

The Soul being then oppressed with these reflections, oppresses itself still more; sorrow, dryness, and disgust banish all sensible satisfactions from the Soul. The more it dwells on these reflections, and thinks that it cannot escape the wrath of God, so much the more it loves God, without being sensible that it loves Him: and by how much greater is the horror which it entertains for sin, so much the more does it persuade itself that it is infected with it.

Then it is that a kind of spiritual darkness spreads itself over the Soul and obscures the understanding. God, whose very nature is mercy, appears then only as a God of infinite justice. A God who is infinitely amiable, appears to be a God of severity, terrors, and vengeance. A God who is always ready to pardon penitent sinners, appears as a God who is ready to punish them for their crimes. And a God who makes use of this subtraction of consolation only as a means to prove the humility and fidelity of His servants, appears as a God who casts off and abandons them.

These terrors pass from the imagination into the heart of a man: the storms of trouble and anxiety begin to arise, the terrors of eternity make a deep impression on his soul: all his thoughts seem to be full of horrors, desolation, and anguish; and all his strength being exhausted by these terrors and apprehensions, the soul seems to fall into a kind of agony. But in this very moment, when he thinks himself upon the very brink of everlasting perdition, the trial ceases: God dissipates the clouds of darkness, restores a calm, and affords peace, comfort, and strength to the afflicted soul.

It is in this manner that Jesus Christ has made those chosen souls to drink of the chalice of the sufferings which he endured in the Garden of Olives, whom he afterwards conducted to Mount Calvary, that they might die with him, and be crucified to the world, and the world to them. It was by this hard, this severe, but salutary proof of their fidelity, that God conducted Job, David, and Jeremiah; and in these latter ages St. Teresa, St. Ignatius of Loyola, and St. Francis de Sales.

Benedict Joseph was called to pass successively through these different states of the interior and spiritual life, and to arrive at a union with God by the means of prayer and contemplation. It was therefore according to the ordinary disposition which Providence had decreed for the progress of souls called to perfection, that he underwent this trial: his faith and submission to the will of God had already been exercised for some years, and was one of the principal means which God made use of to ground him well in humility, and to augment his inclination to the austerities of a penitential and mortified life.

It is principally to this cause that his departure from the Carthusian Convent of Longuenesse is to be attributed. For notwithstanding the rigorous exactness with which the Rule of S. Bruno is observed in that house, it appeared still too mild and easy to this humble penitent; who, smitten with the fear of the judgments of God, and reckoning himself one of the greatest of sinners, imagined he should not be able to save his soul unless he embraced an order more austere. Possibly also a sedentary life, and such a profound retirement, did not suit his constitution and disposition, which was naturally lively and active. Be that as it may, the interior anguish which he experienced, and the hopes of one day obtaining his admission into the Abbey of La Trappe, renewed all his former ideas and affection for that House, and inclined him to think that God had not called him to make his

Religious Profession in this of Longuenesse. He therefore left it after having gone through six weeks of his noviceship.

His first care was to go and relate all that had passed to his confessor, to give him an account of the little success he had experienced in his attempt, and of the state of his dejected and afflicted soul. The zealous Director who was well experienced in the ways of God, and in the direction of Souls, soon delivered him from his troubles and anxieties, and restored him to peace of mind; and advised him to return to his father's house, and there wait for whatever Providence might be pleased to ordain concerning him, and put it in execution.

Chapter 9

The Servant of God Returns to Annette, and Experiences New Oppositions for the Space of Two Years

It is said that victory always increases both our strength and our courage. This was verified in this Servant of God, who, having surmounted the temptations with which he had been so violently agitated; after this storm had happily subsided, found that he was able to do all things through Him who strengthened him. For the new trials which he soon after had to undergo, will show how necessary for him was his confidence in God, and that firmness and resolution of soul which was the effect of that confidence.

Although he had quitted the cloister, he nevertheless thought himself called by God to a life of poverty and mortification. This was evidently his vocation. He never entertained a doubt of it: and therefore though he had returned to his parents, he took a resolution of living according to it, by every means that was in his power. For this reason, he immediately began to add extraordinary works of mortification to his fasts and prayers. His mother, whose tenderness and affection for him, rendered her more and more vigilant and attentive to him, soon perceived it, and made great complaints against it. She many times found that instead of sleeping in his bed, he had passed whole nights lying on the chamber floor. She dreaded the effects of this kind of mortification, and exclaimed against a kind of fervor of penance which she looked upon as unreasonable, indiscreet, and likely to prejudice his health. The answer which he gave to his mother when she reprimanded him for it, was modest and full of respect; but showed him to be still firm, and unshaken in his resolution: "God," said he, "calls me to lead a penitent and mortified life: and it is proper that I should begin to fulfill His Divine will."

His resolution of following his vocation to a penitential life was so steady and unshaken, that when his mother one day refused to consent to his leaving her house, through fear that once he was gone, he might not be able to find means of support; he without any hesitation said to her: "Let me go, Mother, I will live upon roots as the Anchorites formerly did; for, by the grace of God, we are still able to live in the same manner as they did."

These fears and complaints of his mother were not long kept secret. She made no doubt, but that by engaging several others to take her part, she should be more likely to bring him to compliance; and shake that resolution of her son, which had filled her soul with astonishment.

Hence it was, that neighbors, friends, and almost all the family, out of a good intention joined together, to raise a kind of persecution against him, in order if possible to make him abandon his projects. They continually blamed his pretended obstinacy in troubling, afflicting, and alarming a family, for which he ought to entertain the greatest gratitude and affection. They represented to him the inutility of so many steps he had already taken, and journeys and trials which he had already made, and which having all tended to nothing, but to increase the expenses of his education, rendered his alleged vocation suspicious. And sometimes, making use of bitter reproaches they endeavored to deject, and deter him, by severe and stinging expressions.

But this is always a weak method of attempting to overcome the constancy of a man who is sincerely humble. Although Benedict was always submissive and obedient to his parents in everything which did not clash with his vocation, yet he thought that his fidelity in following the inspiration of God was not in any way detrimental to the love and respect which he entertained for, and was due to his parents: wherefore, being full of confidence in the persuasion that his first duty was to follow the call of God, he was calm in the midst of the tempest that surrounded him, and never failed to preserve the good humor, and even the gaiety, that was natural to him.

God gave a blessing to this constancy and humility by changing the views and dispositions of his parents. For being persuaded that a longer resistance would only serve to afflict their son, whom they loved, and whose virtue they respected, they resolved to facilitate the execution of his pious designs.

Chapter 10

He Applies Himself to the Study of Philosophy and Church Music. His Conduct While He Was With M. Dufour, Who Was Then Vicar of Ligni, and Is Now Rector of Anchi-Aux-Bois

Benedict, having attained the twentieth year of his age, thought that it was necessary to fix himself in some state of life, and free his parents from any further care or expense on account of his education. His heart always sighed after the Abbey of La Trappe: his desire to lead a penitential and mortified life made him prefer that to every other retreat; but a holy impatience for dedicating himself without delay to the service of God, and his situation with regard to his parents, did not permit him to wait until the age at which he might be received into that House.

His interior troubles and anxieties had moreover again returned and agitated his soul. Benedict, who was humble and mortified, who had passed the time of his youth in retirement, prayer, fasting, and a renunciation of sensual pleasures, still perceived himself penetrated with a lively fear of the judgments of God and looked upon himself as a sinner deserving of hatred and contempt: nay, he considered even his very imperfections, as sins of which he could not hope for pardon, but only on condition of giving up his body to undergo a rigorous penance during the whole course of his life. He looked upon himself as out of his element, so long as he was not in some austere place of retirement; and he considered as lost to eternity, all the time that he should voluntarily continue in the world.

The promise that had been made to him by the Prior of the Carthusians at Montreuil, of receiving him as soon as he should have learned Logic and Church Music, made him desire to be in a capacity of fulfilling these two conditions. In consequence of this desire, he applied to M. Dufour, who was then Vicar of the Parish of Ligny, and afterwards Rector of that of Anizy-aux-Bois, who undertook to instruct him in these two sciences. The Master, charmed with the virtues and good qualities of the disciple which Providence had directed to him, treated him rather like a friend than a scholar: and gave him an entire liberty to follow the plan of conduct, and the exercises of piety which he had prescribed for himself.

The study of Church Music was very agreeable to his inclination, on account of the relation it had to the worship of God; for which reason the young man applied himself to it with diligence, and with pleasure.

But it was not so with regard to Logic. He immediately perceived how little inclination and disposition he had for this science. Notwithstanding all the endeavors of his master to explain to him everything that was difficult in it; notwithstanding all the efforts which he himself made use of to correspond with the goodwill of his master; he was never able to conquer the repugnance which he experienced in himself whenever he was to apply himself to this branch of study. Nevertheless, he soon arrived at a condition of being able to pass the examinations which he had to undergo; but this was not so much owing to his application, as to a certain kind of facility of comprehension, which was natural to him.

Benedict remained three months with M. Dufour, dividing his time almost entirely between prayer and reading; nourishing his piety by fasting, penitential exercises, and a privation of all, even innocent pleasures. For being then arrived at an age wherein it was permitted him to lay down a plan for his own conduct, he made it a law for himself absolutely to abstain from them. From that time, no one could prevail upon him to be present at the recreations, which on Sundays and holidays, are in use in the country parishes, after the Evening Service of the Church is finished.

One of his fellow students once entertained an idea that he should be able to make him break through this plan of conduct and bring him to the place of these public recreations. In order to do this, he urged every argument which his genius could suggest to persuade him and obtain of him to go at least for once, and out of compliance. But all his endeavors proved unsuccessful, and the servant of God continued faithful to the law which he had made for his own conduct.

As soon as ever he found himself sufficiently instructed in Church Music and Logic, he immediately, and without a moment's delay, set out for the Convent of Montreuil and begged the favor of being received into that House.

Chapter 11

He Arrives at Montreuil and Continues Some Time in That House, in the Quality of a Postulant

The Prior of Montreuil, being assured that Benedict had sufficiently complied with the conditions which he had required of him, made no difficulty to receive him into his House, to try his vocation for a time in the quality of a Postulant, before he should admit him to the Habit of the Order. The solitude of Montreuil immediately afforded Benedict a pleasure and satisfaction, like to that of a victorious general after he has sustained a long, a violent, and dubious combat: or to that of a man, who after a long and earnest pursuit of riches and honors, at length finds his endeavors crowned with success. The austerities of the Rule, the length of the Divine Offices, the nightly Vigils, the variety of the exercises which succeeded one another without interruption, occupied at first, all the activity of his zeal; and he here found reading, prayer, retirement, and penitential exercises, sufficient to satisfy all the desires of his soul. A sensible joy which showed itself in his countenance, indicated the peace of his mind, and the content of his heart. This comfort rendered him still more fervent, by a scrupulous assiduity in the discharge of his duties, and of all the observances of the House. But this calm was of short duration. New tempests began to arise: and it was from his own fervor, that trouble and uneasiness began again to take place in his mind.

Benedict immediately gave himself up to follow his inclination to meditation, and took for the ordinary subject of his thoughts, the infinite holiness of God, the greatness of his obligations towards God, and the multitude of the graces and favors which he had received from him. His imagination was lively, and his conscience was delicate and timorous: and as the eye which has been for a long time fixed on the dazzling splendor of the meridian sun, in the moment when it turns again to view the things on the earth, perceives nothing but a kind of confused darkness; so it was with Benedict, who being employed in meditating on the infinite holiness and the infinite goodness of God, on the perfection and purity of his law, and on the greatness of his love for man; when he afterwards came to take a view of his own soul, he saw nothing in it but stains, but ingratitude, and subjects of fear and terror. The same truths, the same interior anguish which he had experienced at Longuenesse, afflicted him again. The Rule of St. Bruno appeared to him to have been made only for Solitaries who had preserved their Baptismal Innocence; but he thought it far too mild for such a sinner as he looked upon himself to be.

His body soon began to feel the effects of this agitation and uneasiness of mind; and he was too lively to conceal it for any long time. The good Religious perceived it; they pitied, consoled, and endeavored to encourage the pious young man to put his trust and confidence in God; but, thinking that he was not designed by God to embrace their Institute, they advised him to leave their House. And accordingly, after a six weeks' trial, he left it on the second of October, 1769.

On the same day he wrote a letter to his parents, to acquaint them with his departure from it. His letter, which is an edifying monument of his piety, describes, far better than we should be able to do, both the liveliness of his faith and the goodness of his heart. It is as follows:

Letter of the Servant of God to His Parents

"My dear Father and Mother,

This is to acquaint you that the Carthusians, having judged me not a proper person for their state of life, I quitted their house on the second day of October. I look upon this as an order of Divine Providence which calls me to a still more perfect state. They themselves have told me that it is the hand of God which has withdrawn me from remaining with them. I now intend to go to La Trappe, the place which I have so long and so earnestly desired. I beg your pardon for all my disobediences, and for all the uneasiness which I have at any time given you. I beg that both of you will give me your blessing, that the Lord may accompany me. I will not fail to pray to our good God for you all the days of my life: and I particularly request that you will not be uneasy on account of me. Above all things, take care of the instruction of my brothers and sisters, and particularly of my Godson. By the grace of God I shall henceforth put you to no further expense; nor shall I give you any more uneasiness. I recommend myself to your prayers. I am at present well; and have not given any money to the servants of the House; nor did I depart until after I had frequented the holy Sacraments. Let us serve God well, and He will never abandon us. Be particularly attentive to the salvation of your soul. Read the works of Père l'Aveugle, and take care to practice what he teaches. This is a book which points out the road to heaven; and without doing what it says, salvation is not to be obtained. Meditate well on the dreadful torments of hell, which the damned will endure for an endless eternity, and which will be the punishment, even of any one mortal sin, which is so easily committed. Endeavor to be of the small number of the Elect. I return you thanks for all the goodness you have shown to me, and for all the good offices you have done for me, for which I hope God Himself will reward you. Procure for my brothers and sisters the same education you have given me; this is the means to make them hereafter happy in heaven: but without instruction they will not be able to save their souls. I assure you that you are now rid of me. I have indeed cost you a great deal; but be assured that by the grace of God I will make the best use of, and reap benefit from, all that you have done for me. Be not afflicted that I have left the Carthusians; for it is not lawful to resist, or repine at the will of God, who has ordained this for my greater good and for the salvation of my soul. I beg you will give my compliments to my brothers and sisters: give me your blessing, and I will never give you any cause of uneasiness. That good God, whose sacred Body and Blood I received before I came away, will be my guide, and assist me in the undertaking which He Himself has inspired. I will always have the fear of God before my eyes, and the love of Him reigning in my heart. I very much hope to be received at La Trappe; but if I should fail there, I am assured that at the Abbey of Sept-Fonts, being less severe, they receive persons younger: but I think I shall be received at La Trappe."

He goes from Montreuil to La Trappe, and from thence to the Abbey of Sept-Fonts, where he is admitted. The time of his continuing there, and his departure from this last Monastery

God preserved His Servant from despondency, by always permitting him to hope that at La Trappe he should at length find a place of retreat and rest. His humility, which made him look upon himself as a sinner who is under a necessity of doing great penance for his sins, inclined him to think that he should not be able to save his soul unless he embraced that religious order which was of all the most austere. On the other hand, his confidence in God, whom he looked on as a God of infinite mercy and who desires not that any sinner should perish, would not permit him to doubt but that if he persevered, God would be pleased to grant his desires. The Rule of the Order of La Trappe was the most rigid of any that he knew; he was therefore in a manner assured that God, who had proportioned everything according to the wants of His creatures, had provided this solitary resource for the relief of great sinners. And being animated with this comfortable reflection, he set out a second time, and made all possible haste towards La Trappe.

But God had prepared a new trial of his servant's humility and perseverance by a new refusal: he presented himself a second time for admittance, but presented himself in vain. The gate of this retreat therefore was from that time forever shut against him.

But God never permits any man to be tempted beyond what he is able to endure. The servant of God, being firm in this persuasion, and entertaining in his soul an unshaken confidence in the divine goodness, like Abraham hoped against all hope. Sept-Fonts was the place which now remained for him to try wherein to get admittance. And notwithstanding the excessive fatigue which he had undergone, the length of the journey, and the continual rains, which had made the roads almost impassable; he departed a second time from La Trappe, and arrived at Sept-Fonts so soon, that on the 28th of October he was admitted to take the habit of a choir novice by the name of Brother Urban.

He would have preferred the Abbey of La Trappe, because he thought that the rule of Sept-Fonts was too mild. But he was very happy, and looked upon the refusal of his admission into that house as the effect of a particular mercy of God in his favor, when he found that the Monastery of Sept-Fonts was in no respect behindhand with that of La Trappe: but on the contrary, that in many things it even surpassed it in austerity and strictness of discipline.

He passed eight months in the exercises of the noviceship; he was pious, obedient, and laborious, and discharged every duty with punctuality and exactness proceeding from a holy emulation: but the interior troubles and anguish which he had before experienced, returning again; a two-month sickness which had exhausted all his strength; and the well-grounded fears which his Superiors entertained, that being of a weak constitution, his zeal surpassed his corporal abilities, and that he had not sufficient strength to endure the austerities of their Institute: all concurred to manifest what was the will of God, who had permitted such invincible obstacles to be opposed to his desires.

On the second of July 1770, he quitted the Monastery of Sept-

Fonts, and now resolved to go to Italy, in hopes of being there admitted into one of the like kind of Monasteries, where he was informed the lives of the Religious were very regular, and the rules very austere.

Let us now stop, and make a few moments' reflection on him, and his situation, at this important period. If we consider him according to our ordinary way of judging of things, his situation will appear to be truly distressing and afflicting. How many steps had he taken, and how many labors had he undergone apparently in vain! The long and ardent wishes which he had entertained from his most tender age, and which every day increased more and more, the nature of his dispositions, his inclinations, and his virtues; the plan of his studies, and of his exercises of piety, constantly directed and tending to this point; the fervor and perseverance of the prayers which he offered up to God in order to know his vocation; the expenses of an education prolonged beyond the usual term; and in a word, the whole life of Benedict even from his infancy had always been a preparation for a religious state, and a kind of a continual noviceship. This was the precious pearl for which he had sold all that he had; he had relinquished his patrimony; resisted the wishes, and gained victories over the tenderness of his parents, which at the same time cut him to the heart. And nevertheless, he appears to be now reduced to a situation in which he seems to know not what to do, or whither to go. Yet this was the situation in which he found himself at twenty-two years of age, after having made so many journeys, gone through so many fatigues and labors, relinquished all that he had, or had reason to expect, and made so many attempts to be admitted to a religious state.

Having a long time before quitted his father's house, he could not even think of returning to it again. He feared that such a step would be a kind of injustice, by making himself a burden to a family already tired with the great expenses they had been at on his account. His health being impaired, and his constitution weakened, he was little fit for the cloister, and still less fit for the world: he was destitute of the means of getting a livelihood, destitute of support, of a friend to help him, or of an earthly comfort; and at the same time overwhelmed with fears and anguish of mind. This is a faithful representation of his situation at that time. But why should we fear for the just man whom God purifies in the furnace of afflictions? God tries the just, but He never abandons them; and His divine Providence watches over His elect with a particular care, even at the very time when He seems to have forsaken them. It was therefore from the very source, and in the very height of his troubles, that God was pleased to make peace arise, and shine upon him; and sent him a ray of comfort, which thenceforward never ceased to direct and fix him in that state of life to which He called him.

During the whole course of his life, he had endeavored to know and to fulfill the will of God; and we may say that this was the only object he had in view. From this moment, therefore, he began to know what was the will of God in his regard; and from this moment, he began to be happy. He was now persuaded in his own mind that if it was not the will of God that he should enter into a Monastic State, at least it was His divine will that he should, even remaining in the world, practice that renunciation of the world, that interior solitude and recollection, that self-denial, that life of prayer, that poverty, the penitential austerities, and every other virtue which is practiced by those who are engaged in a Monastic state.

In order to put him in a way of following the extraordinary vocation to which God called him, it was highly proper to furnish him with able masters, with instructions, with examples, and with patterns for his imitation, and in order to procure these advantages for him, God had conducted him into different places of religious retirement. And as Benedict had actually found all these things united in the different monasteries into which he had been received, he looked upon this disposition of Divine Providence as a singular favor which deserved to be repaid with the utmost gratitude of his heart.

Benedict, being now persuaded of what were the designs of God concerning him, now gave himself no further uneasiness concerning the means which God would make use of to accomplish what He had ordained: he therefore resigned himself up without reserve to the disposition of His divine Providence: resolved to follow the conduct, the light, and inspirations of His Holy Spirit; and to submit himself to all the sufferings and afflictions which might await him; without asking, or desiring anything, but to carry the Cross, and to drink of the Chalice of the sufferings of his Divine Redeemer.

It is therefore in this new career of merits and virtues, which we have now to consider this Servant of God.

Chapter 12

Pilgrimages Undertaken by Benedict Joseph Labre

A ll men are called upon to lead a good and holy life, as a means to obtain everlasting happiness. And as in the house of God there are many mansions, so likewise there are different ways of arriving at it. For besides the common and ordinary roads to heaven, there are some which are extraordinary, and some singular; but it would be great rashness to attempt to go by these without evident signs of divine inspiration, and of a vocation to them which has been maturely considered, and examined. I am now going to speak of the devotion known by the name of Pilgrimages, in which this Servant of God spent a great part of his life: and in which he behaved in such a manner, as leaves no room to doubt, that what would be for the generality of Christians a temptation to remissness and dissipation, was to him a means of increasing his merits, an exercise of penance, and a means of promoting the sanctification of his soul.

Without doubt, as soon as he found himself in the particular circumstances in which he was when he quitted the Abbey of Sept-Fonts: at a distance from the place of his birth, disengaged from the world and all that was in it, and finding his design of consecrating himself to God in a Monastic State opposed by innumerable obstacles; his love of humility, poverty, and a penitential life, presented to his zealous mind the practice of that kind of piety which he afterwards put into execution.

Rome, which is the capital and only center of the Catholic Church; a place rendered sacred by the triumphs and the tombs of the glorious Apostles St. Peter and St. Paul; and so famous for its monuments of religion and the spiritual treasures which it enjoys and dispenses to the faithful was the principal place and object of the pilgrimages of this Servant of God. Wherefore, from the moment of his departure from the Abbey of Sept-Fonts in 1770, he formed in his mind a resolution to make a journey thither; and immediately began to put it in execution.

Being arrived at Guiers in Piedmont, he wrote a letter to his father and mother, acquainting them with the reason which hindered him from remaining all his life in that monastery. That letter contained in some sort his last farewell to his family; and indeed, from that time his parents never received any account of him till after his death.

The following is a copy of the second and last letter which he sent to his parents.

"My dear Father and Mother,

"You have heard that I have left the Abbey of Sept-Fonts, and without doubt you are uneasy and desirous to know what route I have taken, and what kind of life I intend to lead. It is to discharge my duty in this regard, and to remove your uneasiness, that I now write to you. I must therefore acquaint you that I left Sept-Fonts on the second of July. I had a fever when I came out of Sept-Fonts, which left me on the fourth day after, and I am now going to Rome.

I have now got almost halfway thither. I have not traveled very fast since I left Sept-Fonts, on account of the excessive hot weather which there always is in the month of August in Piedmont, where I now am, and where I have been on account of a little complaint, detained for the space of three weeks in a hospital where I was kindly treated. In other respects, I have been very well since I left Sept-Fonts. There are in Italy many monasteries where the religious live very regular and austere lives. I design to enter into one of them, and I hope that God will prosper my design. I know that there is one of those monasteries of the order of La Trappe, the abbot of which has written to an abbot in France, acquainting him that if any Frenchmen have a mind to go thither, he will receive them, because he is in want of subjects. I have taken out very good certificates from Sept-Fonts. Do not make yourselves uneasy on my account. I will not fail to write to you from time to time. And I shall be glad to hear of you and of my brothers and sisters; but this is not possible at present, because I am not yet settled in any fixed place. I will not fail to pray for you every day. I beg you will pardon me for all the uneasiness that I have given you; and that you will give me your blessing, that God may favor my designs. It is by the order of Providence that I undertake the journey which I now make. Labor diligently for the salvation of your souls, and take care of the education of my brothers and sisters. Watch over their conduct; and meditate on the eternal torments of Hell, and on the small number of the Elect. I am very happy with having under-taken my present journey. I beg you will give my compliments to my grandmother, my grandfather, my aunts, to my brother James, to all my brothers and sisters, and to my uncle Choise-Francis. I am going into a country which is a good country for travelers. I am obliged to pay the postage of this to France. Again asking your blessing, and your pardon for all the uneasiness that I have given you, I subscribe myself,

Roziers in Piedmont,

Aug. 31, 1770.

Your most affectionate son,

Benedict Joseph Labre.

From Piedmont, he with truly edifying piety visited all the churches which lay in his way to Loreto, where he arrived in the month of November: his tender devotion to the Blessed Virgin, whom he looked upon as his mother, and the great favors he had received from God, which he considered as obtained by her intercession, made him entertain a very particular affection and predilection for this famous place all the rest of his life.

After this, he went to Assisi, which is famous for being the birthplace of St. Francis. Here he performed his devotions, and was admitted into the Confraternity established in this place in honor of that Saint; and according to custom, received a small blessed cord which he constantly wore, and which was found about him when his clothes were taken off after his death.

Having arrived at Rome for the first time in the beginning of December, he was for three days admitted into the Hospital of St. Louis, which is there established for the reception of French pilgrims.

Rome, without doubt, presents a prospect capable of enkindling a lively devotion in any truly religious soul; but it would be necessary to be animated with the spirit of Benedict Joseph Labre, to be able to describe the lively sentiments of piety which he experienced, the fervor of devotion with which he visited all the holy places, the effusions of gratitude and love for Jesus Christ and His Blessed Mother, and the tears of compunction, of sensibility, and joy which he shed in the presence of the Tomb of the Holy Apostles.

After remaining between eight and nine months principally in Rome, he undertook a second journey to Loreto, where he arrived about the middle of September 1771.

In the preceding month of June, he had been to Fabriano, to visit the tomb of St. Romuald, founder of the Order of Camaldolese, who had been famous for his great virtues, but particularly for a long practice of extraordinary austerities.

He passed fifteen days in this place of devotion, where he was more and more confirmed in his resolution of passing his life in a state of rigorous poverty and penance. And it was in consequence of this resolution, and to purify his soul from all affection to sin, that he desired for the third time to make a general confession. M. Pagetti,

Rector of Fabriano to whom he applied for that purpose, in this manner relates this particular of his life.

"The pious pilgrim having come into the sacristy to look for me after the Mass was finished, earnestly desired I would do him the favor to hear his general confession at any time when I should be at leisure. I could not refuse him that comfort, after he had shown so great a desire for it. Two or three days after this, going to the church with this intention, and finding that he had properly prepared himself for it, I heard his confession which he made of his whole life beginning from the day in which he made his confession to me, and, going back from one period of time to another, till he came to his most tender youth. In his Confession I admired the goodness of God, and the graces with which He had favored him; as well as his constant fidelity in corresponding with those graces in every age of his life, in spite of the artifices and snares of the devil, and the temptations to which he had been exposed.

Such was his humility, that he looked upon the graces and favors which he had received from Heaven, as only the effects of his own imagination. The Servant of God acquainted me with his design of going to Compostela to visit the body of St. James, in whose intercession he reposed a particular confidence. I observed in him a fervent devotion to the adorable Humanity of Jesus Christ, and to His holy Mother, and a great compassion for the Souls in Purgatory. To a great humility and a singular contempt of his own body, which he called his carcass, he joined an unbounded charity for his neighbor: whom he assisted to the utmost of his power in a spiritual way, by continually offering his most fervent prayers to God for the conversion and salvation of sinners; and though he was poor himself, he gave all that he had in alms to the poor, reserving for himself only the smallest portion, of what was given to him, and such as was scarce sufficient for his support for the present day without keeping anything for the morrow."

Such was the conduct of this pious pilgrim at Fabriano, to which he constantly adhered from the time in which God inclined him to follow this kind of life.

M. Pagetti adds that the inhabitants of Fabriano, being struck with his poor appearance and his piety, immediately began to look on him as a saint; and that as soon as he perceived they entertained a good opinion of him, his humility made him quit this part of the country, in order to avoid the marks of esteem and veneration which they showed him.

In the same year 1771, he went to visit the most renowned places of devotion in the kingdom of Naples, which were the Church of St. Nicholas, Bishop of Myra at Bari; the Church of St. Januarius at Naples; the Church of St. Michael at Mount Gargano; and a great number of others.

The Servant of God was again at Naples on the 13th of February 1772, from whence he departed to return to Rome, where he remained until the month of June, which was the time when he went again to Loreto.

There is hardly any famous place of devotion in Europe which has not been visited by this Servant of God. In the year 1773, he was in Tuscany where he made another general confession, which was the fourth he made in his life. There is no particular account of this journey; but there is no doubt but that his veneration for St. Francis induced him to visit the celebrated church of that saint, situated in the mountains of Alvernia.

From the register of those who have been received in the French Hospital of St. Louis, we learn that he was at Rome about Easter, in the year 1774. He must then have remained but a little time in this city; for in the month of December of the same year he was in Burgundy, France.

His devotion to the Blessed Virgin excited in his soul an indefatigable zeal which spurred him on to visit every place that was famous for her veneration.

The winter season, which was then at its height, the great distance of the places, the severity of the cold, the asperity of the mountains which were covered with ice and snow, were not sufficient to hinder him from putting into execution a resolution he had entertained of leaving Burgundy to go to Switzerland to visit the Church of Our Lady of the Hermits at Einsiedeln, at which he arrived in the month of February.

This Church, which is very rich and magnificently ornamented, belongs to a Convent of Benedictines, situated in the Diocese of Constance, about five leagues from the city of Sufa, which is the capital of the canton of that name. Fourteen successive Popes have granted or confirmed considerable privileges to that Monastery. And Benedict always entertained a particular veneration for this place, which is famous for the great concourse of pilgrims who go thither from all parts of the world.

From Einsiedeln he went to visit some parts of Germany, and in particular Waldshut, Hoggenschwyl, Walweil, and then went to Lucerne, from whence he returned again to Einsiedeln, where he remained until the beginning of July.

The circumstance of the Jubilee of the year 1775 induced him to go from Einsiedeln to Rome, where he continued during the remainder of that holy year.

In the month of February 1776, he for the fifth time made a pilgrimage to Loretto. He set out notwithstanding it was then the depth of winter; and he undertook his third journey to Einsiedeln, which he happily accomplished; and in the course of that route, he again visited several of the famous places of devotion in Germany, particularly that of Waldshut upon the Rhine, where he was on the 20th of August 1776.

His return to Rome in the same year finished all his pious circumambulations; and for the remainder of his life, he took up his residence in that capital, from whence he did not depart, but only to go once every year to pass a few days at Loreto, to render to the Blessed Virgin in her own house which she inhabited on earth, his annual tribute of gratitude and love.

After having given an account of the different journeys of this pious pilgrim, it cannot be improper to make a few reflections on the merit of Pilgrimages, which we borrow from M. Alegiani. They certainly have been practiced by a great number of holy persons. The illustrious author of the book entitled *The Imitation of Jesus Christ*, says with a great deal of truth, that those who give themselves up to a wandering life very seldom become more holy. And in reality, if we consider the life of pilgrims in a certain light, we shall find that they are exposed to a thousand risks and a thousand spiritual dangers, on account of the variety of persons with whom they meet, and the places through which they pass, and where they stop. They expose their mind to the danger of distractions, of curiosity, and of the search after novelties; all of which are things that either extinguish the fervor of devotion or at least considerably weaken it.

But if pilgrimages are looked on in another point of view, it cannot be denied that the life of a Pilgrim may be a means of sanctifying his soul: because it perfectly disengages him from all attachment to the conveniences of this world which he might enjoy by residing in a fixed place.

Who is there that is not acquainted with this evangelical maxim: that by how much more the soul is disengaged from the things of this world; so much more it is raised towards Heaven? To which we may add this consideration that the very places themselves, the tombs of the saints which they go to visit, naturally inspire them with certain sentiments of veneration, which at the same time, excites in their souls a confidence of obtaining from God by their intercession, the graces and favors of which they stand in need, and for which they petition.

If pilgrimages thus, considered in themselves may contribute to the sanctification of those who undertake them, what may we not say of those of Benedict who, abandoning his country, exposing his health to danger, and renouncing the conveniences of life, undertook this kind of penitential life, and travelled alone, unknown, on foot, and without provision for his journeys; accompanied only by his virtues: suffering from the heat of the sun, the severity of the cold, and the other inclemencies of the weather, and by a thousand other inconveniences and dangers inseparable from those kinds of journeys.

Some facts relative to these pilgrimages give us to understand how great was his humility, his evangelical poverty, his disengagement from all affection to earthly things, his spirit of penance, his modest comportment, his love of prayer, and his care to avoid everything which might make him lose sight of the presence of God.

Benedict, having one day asked M. Mancini, administrator of the house called the Hospitium Evangelicum, for leave to set out on his pilgrimage to Loretto; this gentleman thought it would be a satisfaction to him to recommend a companion for his journey, a poor man belonging to the same house, who was a man of a virtuous and edifying life. But the Servant of God begged to be excused from accepting the proposed companion, alleging as a reason for his refusal, his fear that the company of another pilgrim, however good a man he might be in himself, might be to him an occasion of some hindrance or distraction, and withdraw him from that inward recollection and uninterrupted prayer, which he always practiced all the time he was traveling.

Mr. Zaccarelli, his friend and benefactor, having offered him some money for his expenses on his journey to Loretto, Benedict refused to accept any part of it, alleging as his reason, that he had in his possession a piece of money of the value of ten sous, or five pence English; and that this sum was sufficient for him at present. Animated by the same spirit of Evangelical poverty, he at first refused a pair of shoes which the same M. Zaccarelli offered him. But this gentleman pressing him to accept them, at the same time showed him three other pairs of shoes which had been used; Benedict therefore at length yielded to the solicitations of his benefactor and accepted a pair, but chose those which had been most worn.

As he used to wear a straw hat, which was all unsewn and torn, they had all imaginable difficulty to prevail upon him to accept another which was a little better, though that itself was very old and in a bad condition.

From the enquiries that have been made, and the information that has been given at Loretto, we learn some other particulars of his conduct, which are no less edifying than those which have been already mentioned.

M. Verdelli, Clerk of the Chapel in that famous Church of Loretto, and whose business it is to superintend the lamps that are kept constantly lighted, deposes, that he was penetrated with admiration, when he beheld the respectful countenance of this pilgrim; his continual prayer, and the profound humility with which he presented himself in the presence of God in His Temple.

Mr. Valeri, the sacristan, gives the same testimony, and moreover adds, that at the usual hour of dinner, when all the rest of the people went out of the church, Benedict, regardless of his corporal wants, went and placed himself in a corner of the church, where he thought he might not be perceived; and there, with a countenance inflamed by devotion, he saw him smite his breast, and by other exterior actions give vent and scope to the pious motions of his soul.

The same ecclesiastic, having remarked the extreme endeavors of the Servant of God to conceal everything which might give anyone a good opinion of him, went and shut himself up in a confessional to watch him at ease through the lattices, and to see him exercise the repeated acts of his fervent devotion.

All the time that this pious pilgrim remained at Loreto, he not only did not ask any alms, but even refused what was voluntarily offered to him if it exceeded what was necessary for his immediate relief.

Messrs. Verdelli and Valeri, having entertained the greatest esteem for his virtues, looked out for a lodging for him in Loretto, in order to save him the trouble of going every night to a barn, at a great distance, where he ordinarily took up his lodging, and every morning returned again to the church. Having found one, in the house of Mr. Sori, they conducted him to it. Benedict accepted their kindness with gratitude. But as they had prepared a room for him with a bed in it, he thought this lodging was too sumptuous for a poor man like him. They then offered him another, cut out of the rock, under the street; this he looked on as more suitable to his condition, and accepted it.

Mr. Sori sometimes offered him some victuals from his table, but he constantly begged to be excused from accepting it. A poor man, said he, ought not to eat such kinds of food as are prepared for the rich; but he ought to be content with what is left at their table. In like manner, whenever anyone offered him a whole loaf of bread, he would never take it; thinking himself unworthy of eating anything but scraps. He entertained the same scruple against all other kinds of food: and in effect never ate anything but scraps.

Chapter 13

The Manner in Which the Servant of God Lived at Rome, After He Had Fixed His Residence in That City

B enedict, who from his youth had had the happiness to understand the meaning of these words of our Savior, *Blessed are the Poor in Spirit*, carried his observance of them to a very eminent degree of perfection. For it may be truly said, that he practiced the humility and poverty recommended in the Gospel, with the utmost rigor. This was evidently his particular vocation: and that kind of sanctity which he embraced, was the most convincing proof of his faithfully corresponding to that vocation.

Some accounts of the life which he led at Rome, from the time he made that the place of his fixed residence, furnish us with a multitude of proofs of this faithful correspondence with his vocation: and at the same time are capable of affording us great instruction and edification.

There is in the quarter of the Amphitheatre of Flavian, otherwise called the Colosseum, near the Street of the Cross, some ancient ruins, and a great extent of walls, half demolished. Having found in these ruins, a hole of sufficient depth to hold him and shelter him in a tolerable degree from the weather; he immediately thought he could be contented with this place for his habitation. And indeed he had no other for several years. Thither therefore he retired every night to take his rest. And being resolved to carry his cross after his Divine Redeemer, and to imitate His poverty who had no possessions nor place where to lay His head: Benedict thought himself highly happy that Providence had prepared a place for him where he might pass the nights in peace and contented tranquility, and be sheltered from the inclemency of the seasons, and the nocturnal dews.

The life of this poor follower of Jesus Christ was the same as it had been for a long time in every place where he had been: that is, a life of continual prayer. Having employed the whole day in this holy occupation, he thought the time still too short. Wherefore, after having passed the day sometimes in one church, and sometimes in another, praying most commonly upon his knees, and at other times standing, and always keeping his body as still as if he were a statue; he employed also a part of the night in this holy exercise. If at any time he quitted the churches, it was for the purpose of going to the Colosseum to be present at the instructions which are called the Evangelical Instructions, at which he failed not to be present every day in the year.

A kind of life so hard and austere, joined with his custom of praying on his knees the greatest part of the day, failed not soon to weaken him, and impair his health: and brought on a swelling in his knees, which increasing by degrees, in the year 1780 threatened him with a speedy death.

A poor beggar named Theodore, who also had the reputation of being a very virtuous and thoroughly good Christian, perceiving his situation, took pity on him, and persuaded him to go with him to Mr. Paul Mancini, who was the Director and Administrator of the Evangelical Hospital, to whom he presented him as an object truly deserving of his charitable care and protection.

Mr. Mancini immediately took the Servant of God under his care, and put him into his Alms-house, which was established for the reception of twelve poor men.

By taking the medicines proper for his disorder, and a more

substantial food, he soon grew well. And now finding himself out of danger, and his health re-established, he made all haste to go and seek his Benefactor, to whom he said, "You see me, Sir, now perfectly cured: this charity, which you have done to me in taking care of me in your Alms-house, you may now exercise in favor of some other poor person who is in greater need than I am at present. I now find myself in a condition of going to seek my support at the door of some convent. But by what means can I be able to acknowledge in a proper manner my sentiments of gratitude for your goodness, and make you a suitable recompense? I do not in the least doubt but my swelling would have speedily brought me to my grave. It is therefore owing to your goodness that I am now alive."

"It is God," said M. Mancini, "to whom you ought to return your thanks. It is He who has restored you to your health. I beg you will be so charitable as to recommend me to God in your prayers, and I shall be very much obliged to you."

"Ah, Sir," said Benedict, "that I will do with all my heart; and will continue to do all the days of my life."

The care which the Abbé Mancini had rendered to the Servant of God during his illness, had enabled him to discover in him a degree of virtue far beyond what is common, and such extraordinary sentiments of religion which all his humility was not able to conceal. This made him entertain such a high opinion of him that, contrary to the custom and the rule which he had made for that house of not retaining therein the poor which he admitted but only for a certain time, or as long as their necessity should require; he continued to admit him to come and stay in the house every night, which favor the Servant of God continued to receive till the year 1783, which was the year of his death.

It is proper here to give an account of two particular occurrences of his life which happened during his journeys to Loreto, and which show how little account he made of himself. M. Mancini, from whom we learn these particulars, kept a literary correspondence with a nun of the Monastery of St. Clare at Montelupone in the Diocese of

Loreto. He, therefore, being desirous of embracing the opportunity of Benedict's journey to that place, sent a letter to her by his hand, in which, among many other edifying things, he said, *"My letter will be delivered to you by a Saint who spends his whole life in prayer"*. Benedict executed his commission and delivered the letter to the nun, with whom he spent some little time in pious conversation, which concluded by a mutual promise of praying for each other for the future.

The nun then read the letter, and having shown it to the other nuns, the whole community immediately came to recommend themselves to the prayers of the man who had been declared to be a Saint.

Benedict, by this assembly and request of the whole community, was thrown into such a state of confusion, as scarce to know what they said to him: and without waiting for an answer to the letter he had brought, he presently moved from off the premises, and went out of the monastery, into which he never after entered so long as he lived.

When Benedict had returned to Rome, M. Mancini asked him for the answer to the letter which he had sent by him to the nun. Benedict replied, "I received no answer from her." And then in a few words he gave him an account of what had passed. M. Mancini then perceived how great was his humility: and from that time entertained a still greater opinion of his sanctity.

In the following year M. Mancini sent by him a letter to a nun of the Convent of S. Clare at Monticchio: but in this he took greater precaution than he had done before. He mentioned the opinion he entertained concerning Benedict, but he recommended to her above all things to take particular care that neither she, nor anyone of the community, should show to the Servant of God any particular mark of esteem or regard.

This letter was delivered with the same exactness as the former had been. The nun communicated the contents of it to her companions. And they were no less desirous of seeing and entertaining this pious pilgrim, than the nuns of Montelupone; but being previously admonished, they acted more prudently. They came to see him separately, one after another; and in order to engage him to continue a longer time in their house, that everyone might have the satisfaction of seeing him without giving him any occasion of suspecting their intention, they ordered something to be brought for him to eat. By this means, every one of them was pleased and edified. They wanted likewise to furnish him with some provision for the rest of his journey; and accordingly offered him several things, but he refused to accept anything that was offered to him, being fully resolved to adhere to and observe the rule he had prescribed to himself, of taking no thought for the morrow.

This time he waited for an answer to M. Mancini's letter, which he promised to deliver to him. The nun gave him an account of what had passed, and in particular of their circumspection; but at the same time, she did not forget to make M. Mancini pay for that circumspection, by earnestly begging that he himself would recommend that community to the prayers of that good man; and in particular that he would pray for them at the time when he should go to Communion.

While Mr. Mancini was speaking to Benedict upon this subject, he perceived the uneasiness which such a request gave to this poor disciple of Jesus Christ, inasmuch as it indicated that they made some account of his prayers: so that he had no other answer than this to give to their request. "Henceforward I will not have any correspondence with nuns. For who am I that I should be able to afford them benefit by my prayers, and my communions?"

Doubtless it will also afford satisfaction to the reader to see the account which Mr. Mancini himself gives of the conduct of this Servant of God, all the time that he resided in his hospitium.

This then is the testimony which Mr. Mancini gave of him immediately after his death. And it is an additional proof of what we have said, that he was almost every moment of his time employed in prayer, and made it his continual occupation.

The servant of God was always very careful to return to the hospitium at a proper hour. If he arrived before it was opened, in that case, while the others entered into conversation when they were assembled about the door waiting for the Guardian, he commonly went and placed himself behind a little column which made a part of the front of the house of the Chevalier Santarelli, which was just by. There he remained all the while upon his knees in prayer, till the time that he heard the door open. Then, going in with the other poor men, he stopped in the first room where the bed was, that was prepared for him; while the others went on and continued their conversation in an inner room where there were ten other beds. All the poor being arrived, and the Guardian calling them to prayers, Benedict went in, and assisted at them with such recollection and devotion, that all the others were highly edified by his behavior.

Prayers being ended, he returned to his apartment, and then began his private prayers, which he continued to say even after all the lights were put out; so that no one ever saw him pull off his clothes to go to bed. He also arose in the night to say his prayers and made a great number of ejaculatory prayers. And the good man Theodore, who was then Guardian of the Hospitium, and who lay near to his apartment, frequently heard him, during the night, say, *"Lord have mercy on me; my God have mercy on me."* The other poor men also frequently heard him repeat the same expressions.

Benedict entertained a great regard for this Hospitium, because no poor persons were admitted into it, but those who lived the life of good Christians, and in which no disagreements, contentions, or unbecoming words were ever tolerated.

In the morning he arose before the hour prescribed, and employed himself in private prayer, or in meditation, till the time that all the community were called to prayers: at which he never failed to be present with the other poor men.

After this he went out of the hospital; and he was always observed to go alone, and saying his prayers, towards some church: and he generally went to that of S. Mary di Monti, as it is commonly called, where he continued upon his knees in prayer till about noon.

Sometimes he divided the morning in such a manner, as to pass one half of it in one church, and the other half in another church.

At noon he went to the door of some convent to beg one of the portions which are every day distributed to the poor. And then going to that church where the *laus perenne* or forty hours prayer was held, and consequently where the Blessed Sacrament was exposed, he there passed the rest of the day.

Before he ate the small quantity which he took for his dinner, he seemed for some time entirely absorbed in God. The Guardian of the House of Charity of S. Pantaleon in the Mountain, says he observed that every time he came to receive the portion and the bread which they distributed to the poor: before this Servant of God would taste anything, he always took the vessel which contained his food in both his hands, and held it up towards heaven as an offering to God, praying at the same time for the space of five or six minutes, with a kind of ecstatic fervor, while the other poor had begun to eat what was given to them.

These accounts suffice to prove that his life was a life of continual prayer. Every day he said the Divine Office; and the time which was not employed in reading books of piety, he spent either in meditation on the sufferings of our Divine Redeemer, or else in saying a great number of vocal prayers, or pious ejaculations.

M. Mancini here relates nothing but what he was an eyewitness of, or which is publicly known. The plain style in which he writes his account shows him to be a faithful historian. He uses neither eulogiums nor reflections. Let us then imitate this prudent reservedness, and confine ourselves to assembling together into one picture the outlines of the constant, uniform, and hidden life of the Servant of God during the time that he lived at Rome.

In the first place therefore he lived a life of perpetual and inviolable silence: never speaking but of God; and holding no conversation with men. In the space of a whole month, scarce could anyone hear him speak so much as even a few words. Whenever he did speak, his answers were comprised in very few words: for he was always careful never to dispense with his law of silence, but only when humility or charity required him to speak.

Secondly, he led a life of retirement and solitude: having no one for his companion but God, nor did he keep any company but with God. He avoided all communication with men, all the tumult of public places, the dissipation of walks, the sight of amusements so common at Rome: living as if he were in the very midst of a desert, although he was in the midst of a city inhabited by a great number of strangers, and which presents to the sight a most busy, changing, and variegated scene.

Thirdly, he led a life of the greatest self-denial: being destitute of everything; disengaged from every earthly affection; and unnoticed by all mankind: he desired no other riches than those of evangelical poverty; no other pleasures than the exercises of penance and mortification, and no other marks of distinction than that of being the object of universal contempt.

Fourthly, he led a life of the most rigorous poverty[1]: he received no succor or assistance from his family, to whom even his very existence was unknown. He asked nothing of anybody but only received with humility what was voluntarily offered to him; and with generous charity distributed to the other poor all that was not necessary for the relief of his immediate wants. He was exposed to the vicissitudes and inclemencies of the weather, without shelter against the colds of winter or the heats of summer, and having nothing more than other ordinary poor: very old garments, very coarse food, and for the first three years, no other lodging but a hole in the ruins of an old wall.

Fifthly, he led a life of the most austere penance. For to this extreme poverty and privation of all earthly goods, he joined an almost continual abstinence and frequent fasts, though his constitution was weakened and rendered feeble. To these also he added nightly vigils and other particular mortifications. And notwithstanding his habitual infirmities, he persevered in the practice of a kind of penance which frequently occasioned the most lively and insupportable pains; and that was by his ordinarily praying on his knees, which laid him under the necessity of resting the whole weight of his body on two painful tumors, which covered both his knees.

Sixthly, he embraced with cordial affection all the humiliations which accompany a life of poverty and penance. His humility made him look on himself as one of the greatest of sinners. It was for this reason, and to make some kind of atonement for his sins, that he chose to lead a life of reproach and contempt: this was his motive for undertaking all the austerities of that extraordinary penance which he continued to practice until his death: this was the reason why he hid himself among the multitude of poor beggars; why he chose to be looked upon as the outcast of the world; why he chose to cover himself with rags and tatters, instead of garments; why he chose to place a barrier of disgust between himself and the rest of mankind, and disfigured the lineaments of a face naturally amiable and attractive, under an abject and forbidding appearance; and in a word, this was the reason why, through a love of penance and ignominy, he abandoned himself to the bites of disagreeable insects, that humbled body which God now glorifies, and at this present time preserves from corruption, and from being the food of worms.

Such was the exterior and public life of Benedict during all the years he lived at Rome: a kind of life which he embraced voluntarily, and of his own free choice. For this kind of life, he quitted his country, his parents, and relinquished a decent patrimony, and all the prospects he had of being settled in an easy and happy station in life. This is undoubtedly an extraordinary kind of life; and though it is not proposed to us for our imitation, yet it ought to serve as a spur and encouragement to our zeal in the service of God, and incline us to shake off that sloth, that delicacy and self-love, which we have contracted by being engaged in the station in which Providence has placed us.

The humility, the poverty, and mortifications of the Cross always appear to be folly in the eyes of those who are worldly-wise. But perhaps the penitential life of Benedict would not appear so extraordinary to us if we did not live in an age of such general corruption and dissolution of morals, which hinders us from knowing and confining ourselves within the bounds of what is really necessary, and inclines us to follow with eagerness all the pleasures and vanities of the age.

Let us therefore cautiously guard against that precipitate pride, which frequently censures what it is ignorant of, and condemns what it does not understand: and before we pronounce our sentence concerning this good man, let us read with attention the lives of S. Paul the first Hermit, of S. Anthony, S. Mary of Egypt, S. Simeon the Stylite, and of many others in the primitive Church who have been a kind of martyrs of Christian penance.

As members of the Church of Christ we ought at least to look with respect upon the life of this holy man, and wait for the event of the solemn examination of a multitude of wonders, which fame has published as being wrought by God at his intercession, and by his means. And which by the prudent circumspection of those to whom this task is committed, will be so nicely examined, that even the very enemies of our holy Faith, will find themselves under a necessity of acknowledging the justness of the sentence they will pronounce.

Chapter 14

Gives an Account of the Last Year of the Life of the Servant of God

T he secrets of kings ought to be inviolably kept, but it is a duty incumbent on us to publish to the world the wonders which God has wrought in favor of His elect.

Divine Providence having ordained that during the last year of the life of Benedict Joseph Labre, I should be the depository of the most secret thoughts of his soul; I look upon myself as obliged to publish all that the knowledge of which may contribute to the glory of God, to the honor of His servant, and to the edification of the faithful.

In the month of June 1782, just after I had celebrated Mass in the Church of St. Ignatius belonging to the Roman College, I perceived a man whose appearance at first sight was disagreeable and forbidding. His legs were half-naked, his clothes were tied around the waist with an old cord; his head uncombed; he was badly clothed and wrapped up in an old and ragged coat; and in his outward appearance, he seemed to be the most miserable beggar that I had ever seen. Such was the appearance of Benedict the first time I beheld him.

When I had finished my thanksgiving after Mass, he came up to me, and with a great deal of modesty and respect told me that he had prepared himself to make a General Confession, and begged that I would be so charitable as to hear it, and to appoint a day for that purpose: he assured me that I might rely on his sincerity because he did not come with any intention of imposing upon me: and had nothing in view but the sanctification of his soul.

These few plain words, and the manner in which he uttered them, immediately insinuated themselves into my heart, and engaged my affection for him. I therefore granted his request, and made no doubt but that he was a good man, and well disposed.

According to my promise I met him at the time we had agreed on. The Servant of God began with order and regularity to lay open the state of his whole life, and even to explain the minutest particulars with the nicest exactness: from the time of his infancy to the present day; and even mentioned some things which were not to happen to him till after his death. He discovered to me both the present state of his soul, and the honors which God had in store for him; with the same clearness and precision, with which (in several subsequent conversations I had with him) he disclosed to me many future events which had been revealed to him.

I soon perceived in the soul of Benedict an extraordinary light, which immediately threw me into surprise and astonishment. By the manner in which he gave me an account of the whole state of his soul, I perceived that he had a profound knowledge of the whole law of God. He spoke with a wonderful order and clearness on the concatenation of revealed truths and the connection of every virtue; the relation they have to the law of God, and to each other; and he explained the distinctive marks or characters of each particular virtue, and the different degrees of perfection which they contain.

At this my astonishment redoubled: I could not persuade myself that a man, who had never studied, could be able to speak on the most sublime subjects in the same manner as if he had been one of the most learned professors of Divinity. I therefore interrupted him, to ask him if he had studied Divinity. "I, Father," replied he with a great deal of humility, "No, I never studied Divinity; I am but a poor ignorant man." This answer threw me again into all my doubts; so that I could not determine whether the knowledge which he had, was the effect of study and his own reflections, or whether God had not imparted it to him by immediate communication and inspiration.

The clearness and exactness with which Benedict expressed all his thoughts, unfolded all the motions of his heart, and rendered them in a manner visible to my eyes; the particular account of the afflictions through which God had made him pass, the graces and favors which he had received from God, and what he had always done to correspond with these favors and graces; the tenderness of his conscience; his singular purity of heart; his sentiments of profound humility; and his simplicity like that of an infant, joined with an extraordinary prudence, all being united and carried to a very eminent degree, immediately fixed my ideas and judgment concerning him. I saw in this poor beggar, an extraordinary man, whom God, by ways which confound all human prudence, made use of as an instrument of his great designs. I perceived myself excited to enter into the views of his Divine Providence, and I thought myself obliged to make a suitable return for the confidence which Benedict reposed in me; and to render him all the service which might be in my power.

The more I became acquainted with his conscience, so much the more I admired his noble and exalted soul, and the extraordinary graces and favors with which it was enriched. God has sometimes revealed to him the fate of my own soul, and my most secret thoughts; and Benedict has many times mentioned them to me. Without doubt Providence had so ordained that the revelation made to Benedict concerning the fate of my own interior might be a certain assurance of the predictions which related to himself, and which were successively to happen to him till the end of his life.

I ought here to add that in every conversation I had with him, he always acquainted me with something that God had operated in his soul, and that these things in a great measure related to the manner in which He would be pleased to render him glorious in this world, immediately after his death.

We have seen that the Servant of God, from his infancy to the end of his life, advanced progressively and by large steps, in the observance of all the laws and commandments of God. But it may truly be said that in the last year of his life, he led upon earth the life of an angel: by an addition of fervor which is impossible to be expressed. He poured out his soul with the utmost humility in the presence of the Lord; his thoughts and his heart were entirely absorbed in the love of God; and his body, which was mortified and brought into perfect subjection appeared to be no more than a skeleton, covered only with a skin.

On Friday in Passion-week, which was five days before his death, I had a conversation with him, which was the last time I ever spoke to him; and this conversation seems to be of so much importance, that I think it is very necessary to give a particular account of it.

It is well known that this day is set apart by the Church for the solemn annual commemoration of the sorrows of the Blessed Virgin. On the morning of this day, he came to the Church of the Roman College, to make his confession. I found him near the altar of the Blessed Virgin, employed in profound recollection and meditation; and his body was in that state of immobility to which he was accustomed when he prayed. I looked at him with a great deal of attention and was surprised to see that, contrary to his custom, he had a stick in his hand. This had now become necessary to support his emaciated and weakened body. See there, said I within myself, and while I was speaking to him, see to what a condition his austerities have reduced him; it will not be long before he dies a martyr of penance. And all the while, notwithstanding the particular regard I had for him, and which he perfectly well knew, in consequence of all that I had said to him concerning the severities which he exercised upon his body; it never once came into my mind to speak to him about his health; much less did it come into my mind to exhort him to take care of himself, and to moderate his penitential austerities.

I continued to speak to him, and at the same time looked at and reflected on his tattered garments, which appeared so disagreeable to the sight; his flesh of a livid and mortified appearance: and I particularly took notice of his right hand and arm; when immediately some thoughts, very unlike the former, arose in a confused manner in my mind. Perhaps, said I to myself, these rags which seem now so disagreeable, may in a short time be preferred to the richest silks: perhaps they may be honored as the relics of a Saint; but, thought I, before these rags can come to the point of veneration, very great and extraordinary events must happen. Oh how great consolation did it afford me! How much reason have I to bless God who is the author of all Sanctity, and who is so wonderful in all His Saints; to be, as I was, immediately after his death, a witness of the eagerness of all the inhabitants of Rome, great and small, from the common people to those of the highest rank; to see and venerate those very rags, and everything else which had belonged to the Servant of God.

In fine, I must add, what indeed must appear very extraordinary, that neither at this, nor at any other time, did it come into my mind to exhort the Servant of God not to be so careless concerning the outward appearance of his body, nor even to free himself from the bites of the troublesome insects that were about him; and which could not fail of being to him the occasion of a torment in its own nature as humiliating as it was insupportable.

It was for this last reason that I always took the precaution never to hear his confession, but in a Confessional, on purpose that there might be some kind of separation between us; but for this time I changed my opinion concerning that practice; and thought it was more just for me to take such a precaution in favor of the persons who frequented the same Confessional, than it was for me to take that precaution in favor of myself alone.

I therefore led him to the gate of the Roman College, and made him go into the Porter's room without anybody's perceiving him; there I sat myself down to hear him; and he being upon his knees, two floods of tears streamed from his eyes; but though his tears ran in abundance, they were not accompanied with any sighs or groans. The Servant of God then repeated to me many things which particularly related to me, and which he had told me at different times before.

I observed that he at this time showed a greater earnestness to make his Confession than I had ever remarked before; but at the same time, I found not the least thing that was, properly speaking, matter of Confession. Peace, tranquility, and consolations overflowed his soul, which from the time of his last Confession had been entirely free from all temptation and from all interior anguish. This was without doubt owing entirely to the goodness of Almighty God, who, having made him pass through a great number of severe trials, had brought him to this serene and cloudless day which fixes the just man in the state of perfection and makes the dawn of an approaching happy eternity shine upon his soul. I ought indeed at that time to have made this reflection; but God, who was pleased that the designs of His Providence should remain hidden till the end of the life of His servant, did not permit me to perceive that Benedict was then come to prepare himself to take his flight to the eternal mansions of the saints.

A new circumstance which then happened might also have given me some foresight of his death. At other times, before we parted, it was always our custom to agree upon a day when he should come again; I was going to ask the question, but he, not seeming to think of it himself, or having his thoughts occupied in something else, the design I had entertained escaped my thoughts, and we parted without fixing on any particular day. I had told him he might go to Communion in any church to which his devotion inclined him; I took this precaution because he did not always communicate in the church where I heard his confession. He gave me to understand, by an inclination of his head, that he would go to Communion in the Church of the Roman College. Having his hands joined together, and making a low bow to me, he left me. This was the last farewell which I received from this poor servant of Jesus Christ.

In effect, from this time I never saw him till the day when by a note sent to me from M. Mancini, acquainting me that he had taken his flight to a happy eternity; in consequence thereof I went to the Church of S. Mary di Monti. There, following a numerous and continual crowd of people, I was carried to a particular chapel just by the sacristy, in which they had deposited the corpse of the Servant of God on two benches, and where I saw him surrounded by a great multitude of people, who were rendering to the body of the deceased the first fruits of their veneration and devotion.

I then repeated within myself, these thoughts which my heart had entertained on hearing the first news of his death: O happy penitential austerities, which without doubt, have carried him with a full flight into the glory of the Heavenly Paradise. We will now proceed to give a particular account of his happy departure out of this life.

Chapter 15

The Death of the Servant of God

I t is a maxim amongst spiritual writers, that as a man lives, so he generally dies. And it is a maxim so true, that throughout the whole scripture we find but one instance, of any person dying a good death after having lived a wicked life. Wicked men often die in despair, because they have lived a life of sin, and loved their crimes: but the Soul of the just man being without stain, and either preserved in that state by innocence, or purified by penance, his death is precious in the sight of God. This is a wholesome reflection which ought to be made by every one who reads the account of the death of Benedict Joseph Labre.

Almost every day, but particularly from the month of September 1782, I perceived that his health was more and more impaired, and that he sank by degrees under the austerities of penance.

The fatigues of long journeys had exhausted his health and strength. He had experienced and gone through the change of different climates, the vicissitude of seasons; he had endured very severe colds, and excessive heats; and had traveled to places at an immense distance from each other; so that his zeal seemed to know no bounds, nor was it to be overcome by any obstacles whatever. This was in the first years of his penitential life: but after this he embraced a course of penance of a kind quite contrary to the former. He gave himself up to a sedentary life, to a total cessation of exercise, and to continual prayer. He never went out of one church, but to go into another; where he remained either kneeling or standing almost all the day, as still and unmoved as a statue: such was the life of Benedict from the day when he fixed his residence at Rome. Nor could his health suffer less from that extraordinary kind of torment, of which we spoke before, which he endured by kneeling always upon his swollen knees: which deprived him of ease by day, and of sleep by night, and moreover in the latter end of his days his body was covered with sores and ulcers.

To these sufferings which he endured with the most consummate patience, he added fasts and abstinence to a most rigorous degree. His whole sustenance consisted in a small portion which he went to receive at the gate of some convent or other house of public charity; but he did not go every day to receive even this. And amongst the scraps that were distributed to the poor, he frequently and by way of preference chose those which were the worst, and least capable of nourishing his body. It is very true that latterly, with regard to his food, I endeavored to moderate his indefatigable inclination to mortification, and ordered that amongst the different things that were offered to him, he should not choose that which he thought to be the worst; but so trifling a mitigation as this was not sufficient to prevent the consequences of his penitential austerities.

The commencement of Lent was to Benedict another motive of redoubling these austerities. He observed the fast and abstinence still more rigorously than he had done in the foregoing years; and at this time, he would not allow himself any mitigation by making use of the general dispensation granted by the Pope. And it was only at the near approach of death, when he found his strength exhausted, that he yielded to the representations of some compassionate Christian and consented to eat some hard-boiled eggs and to mix a little vinegar with the water which he drank.

A body, treated with such severity, could not fail of falling a speedy victim of penance; and the lively affection of his heart at the same time contributed to hasten the consummation of his sacrifice.

None but truly generous Christians can conceive how great is the affliction of a soul which burns with an ardent love of God and its neighbor: when on the one hand it sees the most heinous outrages offered to the Sovereign Majesty of God, and on the other hand sees senseless mortals committing these outrages, running headlong to their own destruction, and plunging themselves into the most dreadful and irremediable evils.

Benedict entertained in his heart a most ardent love of God; and his love for his neighbor was exceeded by nothing but the love which he entertained for God. He saw the goodness of God despised, and his very blessings bestowed on man made use of as means and instruments of offending Him; he saw Religion rent in pieces by heresies and schisms; attacked by infidels, disgraced by the vices and scandalous lives of Catholics; its Sacraments and its Temples profaned; and the sacred institutions of Penance, the Fasts and Abstinences prescribed by the Church publicly transgressed. Benedict continually loved all mankind, whom he considered as his fellow creatures, created like himself according to God's own likeness, and intended to partake of His divine blessings; as Christians, like Him redeemed by the precious blood of Jesus Christ; and as brethren whom God had commanded him to love, and for whose salvation God always inspired him with the most lively and ardent zeal; and it was this love of God and his neighbor, jointly considered with the injuries that were offered to God by infidels, and scandalous sinners, and the foresight of the eternal perdition into which such sinners were plunging their own souls; that cut him to the heart, and filled his soul with the most lively and compassionate regret. Those who knew the heart of the Servant of God, attest that to make some kind of compensation to God for these injuries offered to Him, and obtain mercy, and the grace of a sincere repentance for the offenders, was the motive of his continual fasts, his penitential austerities, his passing the nights in watching and prayer, his undertaking so many journeys of devotion with so much courage and resolution, and executing them though they cost him so much labor and fatigue.

Thus it was that his love of God, and of his neighbor, made him suffer a kind of double martyrdom during his whole life, and at length carried him out of the world in the flower of his age.

Wednesday, in Holy Week of the year 1783, was the time which God had fixed to put an end, both to his penitential austerities, and to his mortal life. He seemed to have entertained a particular affection for the Church of S. Mary di Monti. For, for the space of about eight years during which he fixed his residence at Rome, he commonly went thither at the usual hour of opening its doors, and there he remained occupied in assisting at the Masses that were celebrated, in saying his prayers, or in hearing the word of God, till the Divine Offices were all finished.

On this day after having employed the whole morning in these holy exercises, about one o'clock in the afternoon, he was seen to fall down on one of the steps leading to the door of that Church. The spectators immediately ran to assist him: he begged they would give him a glass of water, which was presently brought to him. He took it in his hands, and with ardent sighs and eyes lifted up to Heaven he devoutly offered it up to God. It was remarked that after he had drunk, he again lifted up his swooning eyes, and joining his hands, he returned thanks to God for this small relief, with a devotion which penetrated the hearts of all those that were about him and moved them to have compassion on him.

Mr. Charles Anthony Maria Rinaldi, who was one of the eyewitnesses of this transaction, and from whom I heard it, related it to me with a heart still glowing with compassion, and with tears standing in his eyes. The Servant of God found himself so weak that he was not able to get up, nor to stand when he was lifted up. Some offered to carry him to the hospital that was very near; others offered him their house; and with a great deal of tenderness desired he would let them carry him thither. He kindly thanked them for their charitable care of him, but excused himself from giving them any further trouble. At that instant Mr. Francis Zaccarelli arrived, who lives just by the barracks of the Corsican Guards, near the Church of St. Mary in Monti, and seeing him in this condition, he said to him: "Benedict, you are not well; it is necessary to take care of ourselves: will you let me conduct you to my house?" "To your house," said Benedict, "Yes, I accept your kind offer." Mr. Zaccarelli, who is a butcher, well known for his good religious life, and his particular affection for Benedict, accordingly procured some people to carry him to his house, and to lay him down upon a bed, with all his clothes on.

They then were under no uneasiness on account of this accident, as they imagined it was only the effect of an excessive abstinence, and that when he should have taken some nourishment, he would recover his strength again; and accordingly they gave it to him in abundance. But by reason of his extreme weakness, this very nourishment, instead of being beneficial, was pernicious to him: and his swoonings sensibly increased. It was then thought proper to give him some biscuit dipped in wine, in order to revive his oppressed spirits: but now he was not able to swallow anything. The Rev. Fr. Pecillo, one of the Directors of the Society of Pious Labourers, was then present, and was the person who had suggested giving him the biscuit dipped in wine. He immediately perceived the dangerous state he was in, and asked him if any considerable time had passed since he had been at the Sacraments: and if he was conscious of anything that might make him uneasy in his mind? He replied that it was but a little time since he had been at the Sacraments; that he thanked God, he knew not of anything to make him uneasy; and that his soul was in peace. We have already mentioned that he communicated on the Friday before, in the Church of St. Ignatius, from the hands of Mr. Balducci; on Palm Sunday he also had communicated in the Church of S. Mary Major, which is a fact we have been informed of by Mr. Mancini: and although we have no absolute certainty of it, yet there is all reason to believe that he had the happiness to receive the Blessed

Sacrament, on this same Wednesday morning in the Church of St. Mary di Monti.

In the meantime, while the Servant of God was approaching his last hour, he had lost his speech and almost lost his senses. They ran to give an account of his situation to the Rector of the Parish of S. Savior di Monti who at that time was also ill, and therefore sent his Vicar to attend the sick man. But as Benedict was not able to give any sign of being in his senses, at any of the four visits which the Vicar made to him, it was not possible to administer the Viaticum to him; and therefore he contented himself with giving him Extreme Unction.

The Fathers of the Congregation of Jesus of Nazareth, who are distinguished by their charity for people in their agony, being informed of the situation of Benedict, went one after another to assist and continue with him for that purpose till his dying moment. The Rev. F. Anthony Lappies, Superior of that Order, was at supper when the news was brought to him; he immediately quitted the table and made all possible haste to the dying man. He was afterward relieved by F. Angelo Pelusote; after whom came F. Andrew Adami, who was present with him when he breathed his last.

The persons who surrounded his bed were desirous to invoke the intercession and protection of the Blessed Virgin in his favor; and for that purpose all kneeled down to say the Litany of Loreto; and at these words, *Holy Mary, pray for him,* this good man, who had always entertained a particular veneration for and devotion to the Blessed Mother of God, without any convulsion or sensible agony, calmly resigned his soul into the hands of his Creator, in the beginning of the evening of Wednesday the 16th of April 1783, being then thirty-five years and twenty-one days old.

His departure out of this life happened at the very moment when all the clocks in Rome began to announce the time of saying the Salve Regina, which is a form of prayer appointed by the Chief Pastor of the Church, to implore the intercession and protection of the Blessed Virgin, for the pressing necessities of the Church.

Chapter 16

Relates the Extraordinary Things Which Happened Either Before or Immediately After the Death of the Servant of God

I t ordinarily happens that all that relates to this world is over with a man when he is once laid in the grave. That is the fatal period both of his fame, and of his hopes. But on the contrary, the memory of the Saints is immortal. It is when they have arrived at their tomb, that their glory commences: and the hasty succession of ages produces no other effect with regard to them; but that of increasing their fame.

This is one of the means by which the Divine Oracles are fulfilled. He who has renounced everything in this world in order to carry the Cross after Jesus Christ, sometimes receives even in this life a hundredfold reward, for all that he had renounced. We have seen that Benedict had renounced everything, in order to bury himself in a life of poverty, humility, and obscurity; and it seems that God has now thought proper to make the honors which will be rendered to his memory, bear a proportion to the humiliations which he practiced in his life.

Fifteen days before the death of Benedict, a Nun who is remarkable for her piety, and who at the times when the Servant of God made his pilgrimages to Loreto, had some conversations with him upon subjects of piety, was informed by God that he would shortly crop a beautiful flower in the garden of M. Paul Mancini. By this garden, she understood the Hospital of the Poor, of which he has the care and administration. The letter which she sent to that Reverend Ecclesiastic was sent before anyone could suspect that the death of this poor Servant of God was so near. At the time of his death, the same Nun wrote again and acquainted him that the flower which she had mentioned before, was Benedict Joseph Labre, whom the Lord had then transplanted into the happy gardens of the heavenly Jerusalem.

At the same time, God gave a similar notice of his death at Loretto. Benedict, during the days which he remained at Loretto, in his annual pilgrimages to that place, was always received into the house of Mr. and Mrs. Sori, who had prevailed on him to accept a little apartment. We will therefore give their depositions word for word, as they are contained in an authentic act drawn up by a notary to serve in the process of his canonization. "In the latter days of the last Lent (say they, that is, Mr. and Mrs. Sori), we were conversing about Benedict Joseph, imagining that he would soon come to Loretto. Our son, whose name is Joseph and is only five years and four months old, then said, 'Benedict will not come, Benedict is dead.' And every time that we mentioned our expectations of seeing Benedict Joseph Labre, he always said the same thing: 'Benedict will not come at all, Benedict is dead.' One day we asked our son how he came to know that Benedict would not come. To which he answered, 'My heart tells me so.' And the same question being frequently proposed to him, always received the same answer: 'My heart tells me so.'" Mrs. Sori, in her deposition says: "On Maundy Thursday in this same year, I said these very words. This is the day that Benedict is to come. I must get his little apartment ready for him; and my son Joseph, who heard me say those words, immediately replied: 'I have already told you that Benedict will not come at all. Benedict is gone to Heaven.'"

What happened in Rome at the time of the death of this Servant of God is by no means less surprising. God, who is sometimes pleased to make infants the publishers of His wonders and of the glory of His name, seems to have ordained that they should be His first heralds to announce the glory of His Servant. Scarcely had this poor follower of Jesus Christ breathed out his last, but all at once, the children of the houses that were near that of Mr. Zaccarelli filled the whole street with their noise, crying out with one accord, *"The Saint is dead, the Saint is dead"*. And on the following morning the same exclamations and the same words were repeated both in the same street, and in the square or broad place before the Church of S. Mary di Monti.

But presently after, it was not only young children who published the sanctity of Benedict; but the people, and all Rome joined their voices, and repeated the same words: *"A Saint is dead."* Great numbers of persons, who have been eminent for their holiness, and famous for their miracles, have ended the days of their mortal life in this great City: but the death of none of them ever excited so rapid and lively an emotion in the minds of the people, as the death of this poor beggar: this excited a kind of universal commotion. For in the streets hardly anything could be heard but these few words. *There is a Saint dead in Rome; where is the place where the Saint died?*

The people ran in such multitudes to the house of Mr. Zaccarelli, that he was forced to permit them to enter; but a guard of Corsican soldiers was called to keep off the crowd, and preserve good order.

The inhabitants of this quarter being desirous of securing to themselves the possession of his precious remains, begged that he might be buried in the Church of S. Mary di Monti: for this was the Church which during his life, Benedict had most frequented: and it may with truth be said, that from the time that he had fixed his residence in Rome, he had passed the greatest part of his life in it. But the Rector of S. Savior's Parish insisted on having him buried in his Church. This opposition which they met with, made them set their heads to work, and they soon discovered that Benedict was an inhabitant not of the Parish of St. Savior, but of S. Mary di Monti. To the Rector, therefore, of this Parish they petitioned for this favor, which he readily granted. And the Rector of the Church of St. Mary di Monti, being assured of the necessary license, concurred with the wishes of his zealous parishioners, and prepared for the funeral obsequies of the Servant of God, which were performed at the expense of his friend Mr. Zaccarelli.

The people, now impatiently expecting the removal of his body, the crowd kept continually increasing, the guard was doubled, and the soldiers who accompanied the corpse kept the people in good order and at the same time composed a kind of funeral procession.

From the moment that the corpse went out of the house, to the end of the burial service, a sight was seen which is very difficult to be described. Some joined their voices with the singers of the Church and published the praises of the Servant of God; others, in a loud voice, extolled the happiness of his dying such a precious death. These shed tears of devotion in abundance; and the others, tears of compunction. The interior grace of God at the same time mixed itself in some manner with the first impressions which this spectacle made upon their senses. Many great sinners perceived themselves agitated and troubled in mind at the consideration of their past lives, and immediately formed resolutions of amendment, to which may God give His blessing, and render efficacious.

These were the happy first-fruits of souls converted at the Tomb, and by the intercession of this Servant of God, who for their conversion had offered up so many prayers, so many sighs, so many tears, so many labors, and so many austerities.

The solemnity of Maundy Thursday does not permit that anyone should be buried at Rome on that day; for which reason the corpse of the Servant of God was deposited in a place in the church which joins to the sacristy.

There was no person in the neighborhood of Mr. Zaccarelli, who knew that I was Benedict's confessor; so that it was not till the morning after his death that Mr. Mancini informed them of it; and this was the reason why I knew nothing of what had happened till

Friday morning, when Mr. Mancini sent me a note to acquaint me with it.

After the funeral service was over, the devotion and concourse of people augmented in a very extraordinary degree. The Cardinal Vicar gave leave to suspend the laying of his body in the ground for the space of four days; and at the same time proper precautions were taken to keep good order and prevent any tumult.

The concourse of people during these four days, instead of diminishing, seemed to increase every hour. People of all ages, states, and conditions, ran, pressed into the crowd, and were confounded with each other. Persons of the first rank caught the eager desires of the people, and augmented it by their example. Some were seen using their utmost endeavors to press through the crowd and get up to the Servant of God, and others kneeling down at his feet; some with an extraordinary devotion touching his body with their rosaries; others kissing his hands and bathing them with their tears: and everyone showing their surprise and admiration, when touching sometimes his hands, sometimes his feet, or any other parts of his flesh, they found them equally soft, flexible, and in a state perfectly sound and uncorrupted.

On Easter Sunday in the afternoon, which was the time appointed for interring the Body of Benedict, the Cardinal Vicar sent to the Church of St. Mary di Monti, Mr. Coşelli, one of the Canons and his Attorney General, as also an Apostolic Notary and a Surgeon. They brought with them a great number of persons to be witnesses of their proceedings, who by their quality, age, and condition were thoroughly capable of attesting and giving authenticity to the acts which they should have to draw up, in consequence of the most rigorous examination. And by the particular account of their proceedings, everyone may see with what wisdom and prudence they executed their commission.

It appears evident both from the information which they took, and from their own observations, and experiments many times repeated both by them, and by the witnesses, that the body did not exhale the least disagreeable smell or show any sign of putrefaction; but on the contrary, that the flesh was perfectly flexible and elastic in the same manner as is the flesh of a living man who is in a state of good health.

We have judged it proper here to relate several other particularities relative to the flexibility and incorruption of the body of Benedict, though without pretending to have them considered as absolutely miraculous, unless they should hereafter acquire that certainty and authority, in consequence of a more thorough and perfect investigation and examination of the facts.

We have before mentioned the two tumors or swellings which covered both the knees of the Servant of God; as likewise the cause from whence those swellings arose; and the excruciating pains which he must necessarily have suffered in consequence of these swellings.

God put it into their minds immediately to examine these swellings, in the knees of Benedict. They found the two swellings were like two globes of a considerable size; but the flesh was so flexible and elastic, that when anyone had pressed them with his finger, he saw them immediately return to their original form of themselves, and that by the mere action of the muscles. This phenomenon was in every respect like that which is observed in pressing the flesh of a living man. A great number of persons were convinced of this by trying the experiment. And I myself have my own experience for my voucher, because I many times tried the experiment; and always with equal success.

Another thing which we have to speak of, and which seems no less extraordinary, has been attested by many persons, and particularly by F. Francis Bagnagatti, one of the members of the Congregation of Pious Labourers. On Thursday at night the body of Benedict was all over in a sweat, and that in such abundance that his face appeared to be bathed and covered with it. Brother Bagnagatti, who related to me this fact, wiped the face of Benedict with the capuche with which his head was covered. The capuche was thoroughly wetted with his sweat. This capuche I carefully keep in my possession, and it retains very plainly the stains made in it by the quantity of sweat which it had imbibed and with which it was entirely penetrated. The same phenomenon happened again on Saturday and has been certified by many eyewitnesses, who, more fully to convince themselves, applied their hands to his face.

But now returning again to the subject of this narration, we shall give an account of a third extraordinary thing which is still more astonishing than the two former. And to observe the most exact fidelity, we will do little more than transcribe the verbal process drawn up by the Commissary of the Cardinal Vicar at the very place, and at the very moment when it happened, in the presence of a great number of persons who were eyewitnesses of the fact.

After they had, by many observations and repeated experiments, examined and proved the state of incorruption, and flexibility of the limbs and flesh of the Servant of God, they thought of changing his clothes, and putting on him a white habit, which is the peculiar dress of the members of the Society of S. Mary ad Nives, to which society they had associated him after his death. And the body having till this time lain stretched out upon two benches, which being placed close to each other formed a kind of table, in order to put on this habit, it was necessary to lift him up and place him in a fitting posture. Francis Bagnagatti holding him in this position by the shoulders, Benedict stretched out his left hand and laid hold on the board of one of the benches, as if he wanted to support his body from falling after it being in a natural and proper attitude for this purpose. The body was surrounded on all sides by a great number of spectators: I myself was standing at his feet, and then had my eyes turned towards a table where a person was transcribing a note or memorial in Latin which afterwards was to be enclosed in a case of lead, and placed in the coffin of Benedict.

At the noise which I heard on all sides, and the signs of astonishment which I perceived in every countenance, I turned my face towards Benedict, and was no less surprised than the other spectators when I observed the attitude of his body at that time.

Some of the witnesses, being desirous of being fully assured whether what had happened, and which appeared marvelous, might not proceed from a natural cause, or be the effect of mere chance, desired that the body should be inclined a little more to the left side. This experiment was tried accordingly. If the hand and fingers had been no more than simply applied to the bench; if the muscles had not been in a state of tension and real contraction; then when the body was more inclined to the left side, the hand would naturally follow the motion and inclination of the body, and by its own weight loosen and fall lower than the bench; but instead of this, which was natural and necessary, the hand remained fixed to the board of the bench at the same place, until such time as the bystanders loosened it.

They did not confine themselves to this first experiment; they repeated it over and over again, and as often as it was repeated, the same phenomenon appeared. For one of the assistants having required that the hand should be loosened from the bench, and the body placed again in its former attitude: after that, in consequence of this requisition, it was again in a sitting posture; and the eyes of all the spectators were fixed upon the body of Benedict in expectation of what might happen, and I myself was particularly attentive to that same hand: we saw the body naturally supporting itself, in the same manner as we had seen it support itself before; and in like manner the hand holding fast by and squeezing the bench, in such a manner that the thumb and palm of the hand pressed upon the top of the bench; and the fingers were clenched underneath it, the body performing and representing the action and attitude of a living man.

Some time after this, they loosed his hand, and were convinced of the reality of the flexibility of his fingers, and of the extension and play of the muscles.

I add that through the whole length of the hand, of the left arm, and even to the middle of the breast on the same side; the same contractions, and the same play were observed in all the muscles, as might have been observed in any living person, who wanting to sustain the weight of his body in the same attitude, should seize hold of anything that was in his way to serve him as a prop.

By a prudent precaution, the Notary at this part of his Verbal Process set down the names and titles of the witnesses; as likewise the names, and titles, or conditions of the principal persons who were spectators. The Verbal Process, formed in the very presence of the witnesses, was immediately committed to the press, and upwards of eight thousand copies taken off.

Some time after, when they had satisfied the pious curiosity of those who were present, they took off his clothes with all suitable decency, and after clothing him in a white habit, and wrapping him up in a proper and decent sheet, he was laid in a wooden coffin. Many persons who were then without and who had climbed up to a sufficient height to see between the bars what was done in the Chapel, begged with great earnestness that they would lift up that part of the sheet which covered the head of the Servant of God, and afford them the consolation of taking a farewell look at his face.

This request was granted, and at the same time they placed in the foot of the coffin near the feet, the leaden case which contained the Memorandum or Eulogium abovementioned; and to which was affixed the Seal of the Cardinal Vicar.

The body of Benedict was afterwards carried into the Church, and put underground near the High Altar, on the Epistle side. They chose this place in the Church by the consent and leave of the Cardinal Vicar.

The putting the body underground did not in the least diminish the concourse of people. They came with the same eagerness to render to him at his tomb the same respect and veneration which they had rendered to his body whilst it continued to be publicly exposed to the veneration of the Faithful.

On Easter Monday, an immense multitude of people assembled from every quarter of Rome, at the report of the extraordinary favors, which God, to honor His Servant, had bestowed on a great number of people who had implored his intercession. The number of the soldiers that were appointed to keep good order were increased, but all to no purpose. The unavoidable tumult, occasioned by such a great concourse of people, obliged them to give over celebrating the Masses and Divine offices and also laid them under a necessity of removing the Blessed Sacrament from the High Altar to an inner chapel. Some days after, when it was found that the most prudent precautions were insufficient to restrain the multitude, an order came from the Superiors to shut up the church and an express prohibition against opening it for any person whomsoever. Soldiers were placed continually on the outside to guard the door; this new precaution was judged necessary to prevent the heat of an indiscreet zeal.

The order of the Superiors was obeyed, but the church did not cease to be continually surrounded both by day and by night by a great multitude of persons, some of whom prayed on their knees in the adjacent streets, and those who could approach nearer knelt down at the foot of the walls.

The church continued shut for two whole days, and it was thought they might now take off the prohibition without danger of any inconvenience resulting therefrom. But as soon as ever the rumor was spread of the church being opened again, crowds of people began to reassemble, so that it was necessary to form an enclosure around the Tomb and keep off the people by a balustrade, around which a sufficient number of soldiers were placed to prevent any disturbance. This guard was judged necessary, and continued by the Tomb of the Servant of God, for the space of two months.

The news of his death, and the report of the circumstances that accompanied it, and of the wonders which God had wrought at his Tomb, was spread through every province with an incredible rapidity.

The devotion of foreigners now began to unite with that of the inhabitants of Rome. And now a new concourse of people arrived from all parts, and some from the most distant provinces. Some came to petition for temporal or spiritual favors through the intercession of this poor follower of Jesus Christ; others to pay their veneration at his

Tomb, or to return thanks to God for miraculous cures wrought upon them, or for some interior or exterior favors which they declared they had received from God by his merits and intercession.

If we consider well the extraordinary facts which preceded and accompanied these miraculous cures, which fame has published throughout all parts, if we consider the cures in themselves, their number, their different kinds, the variety and great distance of the places where they were performed; and all the other circumstances which prove their truth and their authenticity: how incredulous soever a man may be, he will find it extremely difficult to resist that conviction which naturally follows from the multitude, the authority, and combination of their proofs.

It is true that until the Church has pronounced its decision, we ought to suspend our judgment concerning them. Prudence ought to curb the haste of an indiscreet zeal. And the proofs not having yet been examined and approved by lawful authority, are a sufficient reason for us not to publish them as incontestable miracles. But this at least we may affirm, and that without any fear of being charged with precipitation and rashness, that the truth of a great number of extraordinary cures is founded upon the strongest presumption imaginable.

For of what kind of cures do we now speak? Of cures which are as astonishing by their multitude, as by their variety: of cures of disorders spread through all the members of the human body, and all the organs of the senses; and in many instances, of long infirmities, of disorders of ten, twenty, and thirty years' continuance, and to which some had been subject even from their very birth. We here speak of disorders, whose existence was unquestionable, and whose cure was instantaneous. We have thought proper here to show our reader how long a list of them might be made out, if we were to give a particular account of each of them. For we see that cancers have been cured, fistulas, epilepsies, gangrenes, mortifications, rickets, scirrhus, worms, imposthumes, dropsies, apoplexies, ulcers, consumptions, asthmas, scurvies, blindness, deafness, fractures, and broken limbs.

We speak moreover of wonderful cures, published not only at Rome, but in a multitude of places far distant both from this Capital, and from each other; that is to say, at Naples, Genoa, Malta, Milan, Bergamo, Capua, Perugia, Bologna, in the County of Venaissin, in France, and in a great number of other places which would be too tedious now to enumerate.[1]

We speak thirdly with regard to many of them, that they are cures the accounts of which are accompanied with certificates of physicians, and other intelligent persons, who attest both the former naturally incurable state of the patients, and the sudden transition from that state to a state of health, as likewise the permanency of the cure. And some of which accounts are accompanied with the testimony of the persons themselves on whom those miraculous cures were wrought, and who attribute the recovery of their health to the intercession of Benedict, whom they had invoked to intercede with God on their behalf.

In a word, we here speak of cures that have been performed, not successively in a long tract of time; but such as have been performed in a very short space: and so speedily that it cannot by any means be said that the enthusiasm of one city has been produced by the enthusiasm of the other places where these extraordinary facts have happened.

Accounts of cures were published at Rome in the very week in which the Servant of God departed out of this life. In all the other places, where similar cures have been performed, many of them have been performed immediately after the news arrived of what had been done at Rome.

For the first three months after the death of Benedict, scarcely a week has passed in which there has not been at Rome some verbal processes of miraculous cures, or in which some people on whom miraculous cures have been performed have not arrived to publish at the Tomb of this poor Servant of Jesus Christ, both his fame and their own gratitude to God for the benefits bestowed on them by his intercession.

By a singular disposition of divine Providence, the particulars of his life, from his infancy to his death, have been known, published, and proved in so ready a manner, and at the same time with such exactness, that this itself may justly be looked upon as a very extraordinary thing. From hence they passed on from admiration at the wonders attributed to his intercession, to admiration at his virtues; and these two causes united, confirmed, and more and more contributed to extend the reputation of his sanctity, which immediately was spread throughout all Europe with an incredible rapidity.

As God was pleased to make the glory of Benedict shine every day by new favors, the Cardinal-Vicar thought it a duty incumbent on him to give his orders to commence the preliminary proceedings, which always serve as an introduction to the Process of the Beatification and Canonization of Saints. And therefore, he published his orders to begin the solemn formalities, prescribed by the Popes Urban the Eighth and Innocent the Tenth.

The Archbishop of Nocera was delegated in the month of May 1783, to receive the juridical information relative to those miraculous cures and examine the witnesses who should appear for this purpose and who were to declare upon oath the truth of the facts which they asserted.

The Rev. F. Palma, Rector of the Church of S. Maria di Monti where Benedict was buried, was nominated to do the business of Solicitor in the cause. The Canon Cocelli, Attorney-General of the Vicariate of Rome, was appointed to do the business of Proctor, and Mr. Cicconi, that of Secretary to the Commission.

The information taken at Loreto by authority of the Holy See, and those taken in France, where the Servant of God was born, by the Bishop of Boulogne, have been already remitted to, and received by the Congregation of Rites: and the Process is now carrying on with the utmost diligence and success.

As obedient children of the Church, we ought to wait its decision with respect. Everything concurs to afford us hopes that these words of Solomon will be fully verified in the person of this poor follower of

Jesus Christ. *There is a withered man that wanteth help, is very weak, and full of poverty, yet the eye of God hath looked upon him for good, and hath raised him up from his low condition, and hath exalted his head: and many have wondered at him, and have glorified God.* [2]

THE VERBAL PROCESS.

Begun on Easter Sunday, five days after the death of the Servant of God, and immediately before the Burial of his body.

At the request of Mr. Cajetan Palma, Superior of the Congregation called by the name of Pious Labourers, and Rector of the Church of S. Mary di Monti at Rome, I the undersigned Notary Public, accompanying Mr. Luke Anthony Cofelli, Canon, Attorney General, and Secretary of the Court of the Vicariate of Rome, went about four o'clock in the afternoon to the said Church of S. Mary di Monti, where being arrived, and having with great difficulty entered into it by the little side door, on account of a great multitude of people crowding on all sides. I was conducted into a passage adjoining to the Sacristy, and in the middle of which I found a human corpse laid out upon benches, and clothed with a white robe, conformable to the custom of the members of the venerable Confraternity of S. Mary ad Nives, girded with a cord proper to this habit, having his hands placed in the form of a cross upon his breast, and not exhaling any smell, either pleasant or disagreeable.

Then, the Canon, Mr. Cofelli, acting in virtue of the authority granted to him by His Eminence the Cardinal Mark Anthony Colonna, Vicar of Rome, ordered that to avoid the noise inseparable from the presence of a multitude of people, the body should be conveyed into the Sacristy, contiguous to the said passage, which was immediately executed by the help of the soldiers.

The door of the Sacristy being afterward shut, they proceeded to identify the body, in the presence of several witnesses: viz. Mr. Cajetan Palma, Mr. Biagio Picillo, the Fathers Michael Tricciotto, Francis Bagnagatti, and Camillus Simeoni, (all of them religious of the said Congregation of Pious Labourers), Mr. Joseph Marconi, M. Hannibal Alhani, the most illustrious count, Mr. James Piccini, Mr.

Paul Mancini, Mr. Francis Zaccarelli, and Mr. Peter Sentoli: all of whom, after having seen and attentively viewed the said corpse, affirmed upon oath that they knew it to be the corpse of the servant of God, Benedict Joseph Labre, whom they all knew perfectly well while he was living; and whose soul they now piously believe was received into the mansions of eternal rest, on Wednesday the sixteenth day of April of the present year, which was the day of his death, and which happened in the first hour after sunset, in the house of Mr. Zaccarelli, which is near to the aforesaid Church of Santa Maria di Monti. All of which they affirm to be true and according to their perfect knowledge; they having many times spoken to, and familiarly conversed with the said Benedict Joseph Labre during his lifetime. To which Mr. Marconi added, that he had heard his sacramental confessions for a considerable space of time. And Mr. Mancini added, that he had for a long time given him lodging at night, in the hospitium destined for the poor.

The proving of the identity of the body being finished, and performed in such a manner as to render it impossible hereafter to call it in question: Mr. Coëlli, considering that the sacristy was filled with a great multitude of people, ordered the body to be wrapped up in a sheet, and carried into a private chapel near the said sacristy, where being brought by the help of the soldiers who cleared the way, the body was laid down at full length upon two benches, which had been previously prepared for that purpose: and which by being placed close to each other, formed a kind of table. The body was then measured by a joiner, who found it to be six palms five inches in length. After which Mr. Joseph Chigi, a surgeon, officially appointed for this purpose, after many trials and experiments made by him; found that the body was soft, flexible, and elastic, in all its parts; and had not the least sign of corruption: which was also attested by many other persons who were present, and who convinced themselves of the truth of this fact, by their own experiments.

After they had stripped the corpse of its garments with all proper decency; when they came to change his shirt, in order to do this, it was necessary to raise up his body: which was done by the undertakers Michael Tricisitto, Francis Bagnagatti, and Camillus Simeoni, who placed the body of the deceased in such a manner, that the lower part of his body remained extended upon the two united benches, and the upper part of his body was raised upright: so that he was then placed in a fitting posture. At which time it was remarked, that while F. Bagnagatti was holding the corpse by the shoulders, the body of the deceased seemed to lay hold on the board of the bench, and in a kind of a natural manner to support its own weight.

Those who were present having taken notice of this phenomenon, were desirous of trying whether this might not have happened by chance. For which purpose, they inclined the body a little more to the left side: the hand nevertheless continued to hold itself fast to the bench, until such time as it was loosened from it by one of the bystanders.

The hand being thus detached and removed, the body was in like manner inclined a little towards the right, in order to place it again in a fitting position, when they saw that it a second time laid hold on the edge of the bench, so that it seemed to support itself in the same manner as it had done before: that is to say, having the fingers clenched under the bench, and the thumb and palm of the hand resting upon the top of the bench, and by this means, taking in every respect, the attitude in which a living man would place himself.

Some time after they loosened and lifted up the hand, and found that the fingers were flexible, as has been mentioned above.

This phenomenon was taken notice of by everyone who was present; among whom were Mr. Palma the Rector, the brothers Michael Tricotto, Francis Bagnagatti, Camillus Simeoni, as likewise Mr. Joseph Noel Duvalpino of the Order of S. Vincent of Paul, Mr. Fidelis Relaghati, Counselor at Law, Mr. Marconi, Mr. Mancini, Mr. Mark Anthony Colonna, Mr. Michael Angelus Bove, Mr. Peter Paul de Lunel de la Rovere, Mr. Matthew Angeletti, and several others.

They then clothed the corpse with a new habit, according to the manner of the Brothers of the aforementioned Society of S. Mary ad Nives, and likewise girded it, according to the custom of the said brotherhood, with a cord proper to this habit. And then the body, being wrapped in a sheet, was laid at length in a coffin made of chestnut wood, which had been prepared for this purpose, and which was eight palms and eleven inches in length, two palms and five inches in breadth towards the head, one palm and six inches high towards the head; and at the feet, its breadth was one palm two inches and a half; and one palm and two inches in height.

At his feet was placed a leaden case, tied securely all around with a green silk ribbon, sealed with red sealing wax, with the Seal of His Eminence the Cardinal Vicar. This box contained a memorandum in the form of a eulogium written in Latin upon parchment, which is subscribed both by Mr.

Coëlli, and by myself: and it is phrased in these words:

"In the year of our Lord 1783, being in the ninth year of the Pontificate of our holy Father Pope Pius VI, Benedict Joseph, son of John Baptist Labre, and of Anna Barbara Grandmire, born in the Parish of S. Sulpice d'Amette, in the Diocese of Boulogne in France, on the 26th of March, 1748; after having spent his youth in the constant observance of very good conduct, under the instruction and direction of his uncle by the father's side, who was then Rector of the Parish of Erin in the same Diocese; being desirous of making progress in the practice of Christian virtues, and of embracing an austere and penitent kind of life, entered into the Abbey of Sept-Fonts of the strictest observance of the Order of the Cistercians, and was admitted to the exercises of the Novitiate on the 28th of October 1769. But sinking under the austerities which he practiced in this monastery, a sickness which he patiently endured for the space of two months, obliged him on the 2nd of June to quit the religious habit which he had worn with edification for the space of eight months.

After his departure from the Abbey, he undertook various pilgrimages. His devotion induced him particularly to visit the

Church of Loreto, and the Tombs of the Holy Martyrs S. Peter and S. Paul. After many journeys of piety, he fixed his residence at Rome, from whence he did not depart, but only to make every year a pilgrimage to Loreto.

In every place he gave great examples of Christian virtues, of evangelical poverty which he carried to the highest degree of perfection, living only on alms which were voluntarily offered to him, without asking; receiving only in small quantities what was offered to him, and distributing to other poor people part of what was given to him; he was a man of profound humility, entertaining a sovereign contempt, both for the world, and for himself; performing rigorous penitential austerities; and spending all his time from the morning till sunset in the churches of this city, where he lived, in the exercise of continual prayer. He made himself famous by the practice of all the other virtues: was esteemed and beloved by all, although his garments and outward appearance were neglected and forbidding. A distinguishing character of his virtue was an entire disregard and forgetfulness of himself, that he might make the love and service of God his only occupation.

On the 16th of April 1783, after having prayed for a very long time, according to his custom, he fell down through weakness, at going out of the Church of S. Mary di Monti. In consequence of a friendly offer which was made to him, and which he accepted, he was carried to the house of a reputable man, who lives at a little distance from the said Church. His strength gradually decreasing, the Sacrament of Extreme Unction was administered to him, and, being properly assisted by priests, in the very moment while those who were present were praying for him; he calmly resigned his soul into the hands of his Creator, in the first hour after sunset, of the same day on which he fell sick.

On the morning following, his body was conveyed with all suitable decency into the said Church; and a great concourse of people were present at his dirge, which was performed at the expense of certain pious persons, who took that charitable office upon themselves.

Immediately afterwards, a kind of almost universal commotion communicated itself throughout all Rome, at the news of his death, which spread itself suddenly, together with the fame of his great sanctity. Then, such a great concourse of people of all ranks and conditions began to crowd to the Church, that the soldiers who had been called to keep good order, had a great deal of difficulty to keep the multitude in subjection.

To satisfy the piety of the Faithful whose number increased more and more, His Eminence the Cardinal Vicar gave leave to defer the laying of the body underground till the evening of Easter Sunday, which in this year 1783 falls on the twentieth of April. This same day, by order of His Eminence the body was, about the time of sunset, laid underground, in an honorable and particular place of this Church.

Signed,

Luke Anthony Coselli, Attorney

General of the Vicariate of Rome.

Francis Mari, Notary, at the request of Mr. Joseph Cicconi."

We think we ought here to add some few interesting anecdotes relative to the life of this Servant of God, which we have received from Mr. Alegiani; and which afford us a great idea of his patience, his humility, and the profound recollection of his soul in prayer.

One day as this Servant of God passed by the Hospital Colonna, where some boys were playing at quoits, one of them struck him with a stone on the left leg near the ankle bone; the blow was so violent as to make a great quantity of blood spout out; nevertheless, he did not reveal his pain by any sign whatever; and what is still more extraordinary is that he did not turn about to see who had struck him; but continued to walk on, with the same peace and tranquility as before.

Another day as he was crossing the Coliseum, seeing some boys playing in an indecent manner, he went up to them, and his zeal being enkindled, he gave them a reprimand mixed with a good deal of sweetness: but the boys took up stones and began to throw them at their charitable monitor, as the reward of his zeal. A man who was a spectator of their behavior, ran up to defend Benedict. But the servant of God said to him: *"Let them alone, let them do what they please: for if you knew who I am, you yourself would throw stones at me with still more rage than these boys."*

It was with the same unalterable peace that he endured a cruel insult from one of his benefactors. This man had given him a Baiocco, or Italian penny, but perceiving that Benedict gave it to another poor person, he looked upon this action in a bad light, imagining that Benedict disdained to accept so small an alms: and therefore came up to him and struck him with his cane. After the death of this poor Servant of Jesus Christ, he remembered the injury he had done him; and penetrated with the most lively sentiments of repentance, he ran to the Church of St. Mary di Monti, to ask his pardon, and, as a token and memorial of his sorrow, he left in that church, the guilty instrument with which he had struck him. Mr. Zitli, whose depositions will be examined in the Process of Canonization, was one of the principal witnesses of the respect and reverence with which the Servant of God prayed in the churches. He was in a manner annihilated in the presence of God: having his eyes turned sometimes towards the adorable victim of our Salvation, and sometimes towards the earth, with a devotion that astonished every beholder. Mr. Zitli declares that on one day, he observed him for several hours, kneeling before the Blessed Sacrament, in the church of the Capuchins, and saw him all the time totally destitute of motion: and absorbed in adoration and prayer to such a degree, that he suspected he was dead, and went to him to jog him, and thereby discover whether he was dead or alive.

Mr. Zitli had been Treasurer to Kouli Khan, of Persia. This prince having been put to death by his nephew, Mr. Zitli fled to Astrakhan; and being afterwards, by the Divine Mercy, brought into the bosom of the Catholic Church; and having by his liberal alms, and other good works, stripped himself of the immense riches, which he had brought with him; he is now, at ninety-three years of age, maintained out of charity in a convent of the Capuchins at Rome.

REFLECTION.

How great is the difference between the death of a good man, who, having lived in a state of contempt and obscurity, leaves behind him a bright and unsullied reputation; and the death of the unbeliever famous for his crimes and his impious publications! The first is approved by Religion, only because he has faithfully discharged every duty of the state in which he lived in the world, and is revered or honored by her only because he was so far from renouncing the service of God to serve the world; that whatever he did to serve that world was all referred to the honor and glory of God, and done solely for His sake. The other acquires nothing more than an empty name, which is speedily forgotten when its author is no more. Great in the eyes of the world, he almost disdained to number the just man among his slaves; while the just man upon the dunghill blessed his peaceable obscurity, and thought himself happy in having nothing to wish for, nothing to regret, and nothing to leave behind him on earth, because he knew virtue alone gives immortality.

The infidel was only solicitous to make himself a name; the present was his only object, he forgot that everything perished with a man except his righteousness and his thoughts and affections were constantly bewitched by present objects; he was chained to the earth as if he thought he was never to be separated from it. The just man, penetrated with the idea of the greatness of God whom he adored, became great himself by the constant practice of truth, of charity, of modesty, and disinterestedness; that is, he became great in the eyes of Religion, being ennobled by Faith. But alas! What has now become of Faith? Is not all Europe overrun with books of infidelity and immorality, which Hell has sent on purpose to poison, to corrupt, and to destroy it? To frustrate this infernal scheme, we need only cast a glance at the character of the men who attack this Faith. For while the Christian can have no other interior motive for believing divine Revelation than the love and desire of practicing the virtues which it recommends; the incredulous can have no other real motive for not believing it than the love and desire of practicing the vices which it condemns. But, by what fatality could it happen, that what is the source of virtue should be an imposture, and that light and truth should flow from the sink of vice? What can these Infidels, who falsely assume to themselves the name of Philosophers, oppose to a Religion so sublime in its doctrines and so perfect in its Morality, that if it were the work and invention of man, we might boldly assert that man has been able perfectly to imitate the work of God. This sublimity of the Gospel and the purity and excellency of its maxims, and of the person of Jesus Christ, of whose life it is a summary, is described by one of the greatest infidels of the present age, John James Rousseau, in the following words. "I must acknowledge that the majesty of the Scriptures fills me with astonishment; the sanctity of the Gospel speaks to my heart. Look at all the books of the philosophers, with all their pomp, and you will find them little and mean if compared with this. Is it possible that a book at once so sublime and so simple can be the production of men? Is it possible that He whose history is here given should be nothing more than a man? Is this the tone of an enthusiast or an ambitious sectary? What sweetness, what purity in His morals? What unction in His instructions? What dignity in His maxims; what profound wisdom in His discourses! What presence of mind, what wariness and exactness in His answers! And what command over His passions! Where is the man, where is the sage, who knows how to act, to suffer, and to die, without either weakness or ostentation? When Plato describes his imaginary just man, laden with all the ignominy of guilt, though really deserving all the honor and rewards of virtue; he draws Jesus Christ at every stroke. The resemblance is so striking, that all the Fathers have taken notice of it, and it is not possible for anyone to be deceived by it. How great must be the prejudices, how great the blindness, of the man who dares compare the Son of Sophronisca with the Son of Mary?

How great a difference is there between the one and the other! Socrates, dying without pain and without ignominy, easily supported his character to the last; and if this easy death had not crowned his life, we might doubt whether Socrates, with all his wisdom, had been anything more than a mere Sophist. They say he invented the rules called Moral Philosophy. But others had first reduced those rules to practice; he did nothing more than say what they had done and turn their examples into lessons. Aristides had been just before Socrates had said what Justice was. Leonidas had died for his country before Socrates had declared it a duty to love it. Sparta was sober before Socrates praised sobriety; and before he had defined virtue, Greece abounded in virtuous men. But from whom did Jesus learn that sublime and pure morality, of which he alone has given both the lessons and the examples? The death of Socrates, peacefully philosophizing in the midst of his friends, is the easiest one can desire; that of Jesus, expiring in torments, insulted, scoffed at, and blasphemed by a whole people, is the most horrible one can fear. Socrates, taking the poisoned cup, blesses the man who presents it to him with tears! Jesus, in the midst of the agonies of a most cruel death, prays for his savage executioners. Yes, if the life and death of Socrates be those of a Sage; the life and death of Jesus are those of a God. Shall we then say that the Gospel History is a fiction? No, my friends, this cannot be: for the facts of Socrates, of which no one doubts, are not half so well attested as those of Jesus Christ. And at best, this would be only evading the difficulty, not answering it. For it would be more difficult to conceive that many should combine to write such a book; than that one should furnish the matter. Jewish authors would never have been able to hit upon either this manner of expression or this sublime morality: and the Gospel has characters of truth so great, so striking, so perfectly inimitable; that the inventor would have been more astonishing than the Hero."

Rousseau's *Emile*[3] What, I say, can they oppose to it but some merely apparent contradictions contained in the holy Scriptures which have been a thousand times cleared up and reconciled; and old sophistical arguments which have been confuted many ages ago, and are deserving the contempt of men, even of the most ordinary capacity. If then Faith should be banished from among us; the great crime of our age will be to have quitted Religion; and the lasting reproach with all posterity, will be to have abandoned it without any shadow of reason, or rather without any other reason than that of the violence of our passions. Dangerous citizens, their zeal is as pernicious to public probity as to faith; and to the state, as to religion. Base and perfidious seducers, they constitute themselves the apostles of impiety for no other purpose than to inspire the authors of their fortune and the objects of their passions with weaknesses of which they may afterwards take advantage. They desire to extinguish the light of faith only because they fear the revival of reason and the return of virtue. But their wickedness, well understood, will never be able to deceive any but those who are willing to be deceived. And notwithstanding the unrestrained licentiousness and daring impiety with which they attack religion, it will always take a much deeper root in virtuous souls: as it has never had any other enemies than men in whom an audacious pride occupied the place of knowledge and study, and who were disgraced, vilified, and dishonored by their immoralities.

Wretched stupidity! When wilt thou awake out of thy lethargy? With a heart so tender for creatures; when wilt thou cease to be so hard and insensible towards thy God! We see the world every moment rushing towards its dissolution, the earth laid waste by fatal accidents which threaten it with ruin, and we do not think on that moment which will cut our thread of life asunder.

Appendix

Giving an Account of the Miracles Said To Have Been Wrought by the Almighty, at the Intercession of This His Faithful Servant.

W e read in the thirteenth chapter of the fourth book of Kings, otherwise called the second book of Kings, that the prophet Elisha died, and they buried him. And the raiders from Moab came into the land the same year. And some that were burying a man saw the raiders, and cast the body into the sepulchre of Elisha. And when it had touched the bones of Elisha, the man came to life, and stood upon his feet. Here we see a miracle wrought by Almighty God, by the means of the relics of the prophet, and that, without anyone's petitioning for, or even apprehending the likelihood of any such miracle being wrought in favor of the deceased. After this instance of the extraordinary goodness of Almighty God, it is no wonder that the woman mentioned in the Gospel, Matt. ix. 20, who had been troubled with an issue of blood twelve years, should have such faith and confidence in the goodness of God, as to think that if she should touch but the hem of our Savior's garment, she should be healed. And in effect we find, that her faith and confidence were commended and rewarded by our Savior, by the restoration of her health according to her wish.

We read again in the Acts of the Apostles xix. 12, that "Aprons and Handkerchiefs which had touched the body of S. Paul were carried to the sick, and the diseases departed from them, and the wicked spirits went out of them."

These instances of favors received from Almighty God by touching the bones of the Prophet Elisha, and the Aprons and Handkerchiefs which had touched the body of S. Paul, induced the Christians in the first Ages of Christianity to pay particular respect and veneration for the bodies, or Relics, of the holy Martyrs; not doubting but those glorious Champions who had conquered the devil and the world, by laying down their lives for the Faith of Christ, and were admitted into the mansions of eternal bliss, would obtain similar favors from God for them, or at least present their Petitions before the throne of God, and solicit for them his spiritual graces and benedictions. Hence, we read in the Acts of St. Ignatius, Bishop of Antioch and Martyr, that being devoured by the wild beasts, nothing was left of his body *but only some of the bones; which were carried to Antioch,* and given to that Church, for the Martyr's sake, as an *inestimable treasure.* Ruinart's *Acta Sincera Martyrum,* Sect. 5, p. 707.

When the body of St. Polycarp was burnt, the Christians collected what remained of his bones, and carried them away: which they valued more than gold and precious stones. Eusebius, *Lib. 4, Hist. Cap.* 15, p. 134.

When St. Andronicus suffered martyrdom, the Proconsul Maximus commanded his tongue and teeth to be pulled out and burnt to ashes, and the ashes thrown into the wind, lest, said he, 'any pitiful women of the Christians should keep them for a treasure.' Ruinart, p. 487.

St. Basil says that according to the Jewish rites, all dead bodies are an 'abomination;' but now, if anyone dies for the Name of Christ, his relics are esteemed precious. Then, the touch of a dead body defiled a man; now it almost sanctifies him. St. Basil in *Psalm* 115, T. 1, p. 274.

St. Gregory Nyssen says that a Christian thinks himself sanctified and blessed by touching the tomb of a martyr: and much more if he be allowed to take away any of the dust from the Sepulchre. Orat. de St. Theodoro Mart. Tom. 3. p. 579. 580.

St. Jerome writing against Vigilantius, who pretended that relics were not to be honored, opposes against him the example of all the bishops in the world. Lib. contra Vigilantium.

Again, says he, *"We honor the relics of the martyrs, that we may adore Him whose martyrs they are. We honor the servants, that the Master may be honored, who says; 'He that receives you, receives Me.'"* Ep. 53. ad Riparium. And again, "You write that Vigilantius vomits once more his poison against the relics of the martyrs, calling us dust-worshippers and idolaters, for reverencing dead men's bones. Oh unhappy man who can never be sufficiently pitied." Ibid.

Dr. Burnet, the Protestant Bishop of Salisbury, says, *"It is no wonder that great care was taken in the beginnings of Christianity, to show all possible respect and tenderness even to the bodies of the martyrs. There is something of this planted so deep in human nature, that though the philosophy of it cannot be so well made out, yet it seems to be somewhat more than a universal custom. We think that all decent honors are indeed due to the bodies of the saints, which were once the temples of the Holy Ghost."*—And writing concerning the Acts which give an account of the respect paid by the primitive Christians to the relics of St. Polycarp, he says, *"This is one of the most valuable pieces of true and genuine Antiquity: and it shows us very fully the sense of that age, both concerning the Relics, and the worship of the Saints."* Burnet's Expos. of the 39 Articles. Art. 22. p. 313, 316.

And lastly, Eunapius, a pagan writer who lived in the fourth century, says, *"The Christians, gathering the heads and bodies of such as the Magistrates had executed, made them their Gods, prostrated before them, and thought themselves purer, by being defiled at their Tombs."*

This respect and veneration which was shown to the relics of the Martyrs, and which was referred to and redounded to the Glory of God, whose Martyrs they are, was approved of by God Himself; both by miraculously revealing where the relics of some of His Martyrs were deposited, and by the many Miracles He was pleased to work by their means.

Concerning the Miracles wrought by the relics of the Martyrs, St. Gregory Nazianzen says, *"Did you not fear the Martyrs and Saints, John, Peter, Paul, James, Stephen, Luke, Andrew, Thecla, and so many others—to whom great honor and Festivals are appointed, by whom devils are cast out, and diseases cured: whose very bodies whether touched, or honored, do the same as their holy Souls: and* a drop of their blood, or any little remnant of their Passion, as much as their bodies?" Orat. 3. quæ est 1 cont. Julianum Tom. 1. p. 76. Ed. Paris.

St. Ambrose says, "You have known, nay yourselves have seen many dispossessed, many delivered from their infirmities as soon as they touched the Veil which covered the holy Bodies. The ancient Miracles of Christ are revived. You see many cured, by the shadow as it were of the Saints' Bodies. How many Handkerchiefs are they touched with? How many Veils, by touching the sacred Relics, become instruments of the greatest cures? Everyone is glad to touch the most distant hem; and if he does it, he will be healed." St. Ambrose Ep. 22.

St. Isidore of Pelusium. "If this offends you that we honor the ashes of the Martyrs' Bodies, because they loved God and served Him constantly; ask those who have been healed by them, and inquire into the number of distempers from which they have been freed. If you do this, you will be so far from laughing at what we do, that you will be willing to join with us in so innocent a practice." Lib. 1. Ep. 55.

St. Augustine in his Book of the City of God, relates several Miracles performed at the Shrines, or by the means of the Relics of St. Stephen: viz. 1. A blind woman recovered her sight, by applying to her eyes some flowers which had touched his Relics.

2. Bishop Lucillus, by carrying the relics of St. Stephen, was cured of a fistula, with which he had long been troubled, and was never troubled with it after that day. 3. Eucherius, a Spanish priest,

who dwelt at Calame, was cured of the stone by part of the same relics, which Bishop Possidius carried thither; and being afterwards laid out for dead in consequence of another disorder, by the help of the said martyr, to whose shrine they carried him, was restored to his former life and soundness. 4. A child which had been crushed by a cart, was carried by its mother, and laid down before the shrine of St. Stephen, where it recovered both life and full strength in an instant. 5. A devout woman at Caspaliana, being sick and past recovery, sent her garment to the shrine; but before it came back, she was dead. However, her parents covered her with it; which done, she presently revived, and was in as good health as ever. 6. The like happened to the daughter of one Bassius, a Syrian who dwelt at Hippo: he covered his dead daughter with her garment which he had carried to the shrine, and she was presently restored to life. 7. Irenæus, a collector, having one of his sons dead, one advised him to anoint him with some of St. Stephen's oil; he did so, and his son was restored to life. After giving an account of these miracles, St. Augustine goes on and says, *"If I should write all the miracles performed on men's bodies by the memorials of St. Stephen, only at Calama and Hippo, it would be a work of many volumes, and not be perfect neither. It is not yet two years since his memory began (that is, his relics were deposited) at Hippo, and although we ourselves do know many miracles done there since then are not recorded, yet there are relations given in of almost seventy of those that have been done since that time to this."* St. Aug lib. 22. de Civit. Dei cap. 8. Several other miracles of the like nature are by St. Ambrose, St. Augustine, and St. Paulinus, related to have been performed at Milan, by means of the relics of SS. Gervasius and Protasius; and indeed St. Ambrose in the place above quoted says that the veils which touched those relics had become *"instruments of the greatest cures"*. And for the truth of those miracles, he appeals to those who had been eyewitnesses of them.

Theodoret mentions another practice of the faithful in his days: for he says, *"That those who ask with faith, obtain their requests as appears from the donaries witnessing their cures. For some hang up the* resemblances of eyes, some of feet, others of hands, made of gold or silver. These show the martyr's power, and that the God whom they worshipped is the true God." Serm. 8. de curand Gracor Affect. Tom 4. p. 593, 594.

Since the Almighty God has been pleased frequently to work miracles by the means of the relics of the martyrs, in testimony of His faith and of the sanctity of His servants, in like manner as He had before wrought the like miracles by the means of the aprons and handkerchiefs that had touched the body of S. Paul, in testimony of His divine commission and authority to preach the same faith to all the world: it is no wonder that the Christians should entertain a great veneration for those sacred remains of those servants of God, and present themselves before the tombs of the martyrs, to beg of them to intercede with God on their behalf, to beseech Him to deliver them from their afflictions, and bestow upon them all the spiritual and temporal blessings of which they stood in need: as the Holy Fathers in their writings assure us they did. For St. Chrysostom says: *"He who wears the purple comes to these tombs to kiss them; and casting off his pride, standeth humbly, invoking the saints, that they may defend him at the tribunal of God. And that the tent-maker, and fisherman, though dead, may be his patrons, is the earnest request of him that wears the diadem."* St. Chrysost. hom. 26. in Ep. 2. ad Cor.

And in another place he exhorts the people to make this their constant practice. *Let us not therefore on this day only, but every day visit his tomb, that thereby we may obtain spiritual blessings from God.* For if by touching the bones of Elisha a dead body was restored to life, if a man approaches the tomb with faith, he may with much more reason hope for blessings at present, since graces flow with more abundance. God has given us the relics of His saints, that He might lead us by degrees to an emulation of their zeal, and that we might have a security and comfort against the evils which surround us. Tom. 1, Or 42, p. 507.

And again. *Let us, says he, therefore, not only on this day, but every day, visit their tombs (of Domnia, Berenice, and Prosdocimus, whose* shrines were in the city of Antioch where he preached this sermon) that thereby we may obtain spiritual blessings from God. Let us beseech them, let us beg of them to be our protectresses. For their power was great, not only when living, but is also, and much more when dead. For now they bear the marks of Christ. And when they show these, they may obtain all things from the King. St. Chrysostom. Tom. 1, Or 51, Ed. Ben. p. 570.

St. Ambrose says: The martyrs are to be invoked, whose patronage we have a claim to, by possessing their Relics.—Let us not be ashamed to make use of them as Intercessors for our Infirmity; who knew the weakness of the Body, at the same time that they conquered it. *Lib de Vitiis.*

Mr. Thorndike, a Protestant writer, says, "It is confessed that the lights, both of the Greek and Latin Church, Basil, Nazianzen, Nyssen, Ambrose, Jerome, Augustine, Chrysostom, both Cyrils, Theodoret, Fulgentius, Gregory the Great, Leo; more, or rather all of that time, have spoken to the Saints, and desired their assistance." Thorndike's *Epil.* part 3, p. 358.

And Bishop Montague in his *Treatise of the Invocation of Saints* p. 97, says, "I see no absurdity in nature, no incongruity unto Analogy of Faith, no repugnancy at all to Sacred Scripture, much less Impiety, for any man to say, 'Holy Angel Guardian, pray for me.'"— And again in the same treatise he says of the Saints: "Could I come at them, or certainly inform them of my state: without any question or more ado, I would readily and willingly say, 'Holy Peter, Blessed Paul, pray for me; recommend my case to Christ Jesus our Lord.' Were they with me, by me, in my hearing, I would run with open arms, and fall upon my knees, and with affection desire them to pray for me."

Hence then it appears, 1. That in the first Ages of Christianity the Faithful preserved the Relics of the Martyrs with great care and veneration: looking upon them as more valuable than gold and precious stones. 2. That God wrought many miracles in favor of those who at the tombs of the martyrs touched their relics, and with a lively faith implored their intercession. 3. That the holy fathers, the most illustrious lights of God's Church, bear testimony to these miracles being wrought. And 4. the same holy fathers exhort and encourage the faithful to visit the relics of the martyrs, and to invoke the martyrs whose relics they visit, that they may obtain by their intercession spiritual and temporal blessings from God.

Venerable Bede in the fourth book of his Ecclesiastical History, cap. 31 and 32, gives an account of a man who was in like manner cured of a palsy at the shrine of St. Cuthbert: and of another who was cured of a swelling in his eyelid, by touching it with some of the hair of the same saint. The same author relates in the life of St. Cuthbert, that another person was also cured of a palsy by having the shoes in which St. Cuthbert had been at first buried upon his feet. Cap. 45.

St. Bernard says that after the death of St. Malachias, "his funeral rites were performed: the sacrifice and all things were done with the utmost devotion. At the same time a lad stood at a distance whose withered arm hung down by his side, and was more troublesome than beneficial to him. Observing which, I made a sign to him to come to me. And taking hold of his withered arm, I applied it to the hand of the Bishop; and he restored it to life. For the gift of healing still remained in the dead body: and his hand was to the withered hand, what Elisha was to the dead man. That lad had come from a great distance: and the hand which he had brought hanging down uselessly by his side, he carried back into his own country whole and as capable of performing its functions as the other." St. Bernard in *Vita St. Malachiae cap. 31.*

In every age God has been pleased to work similar miracles by the relics of His Saints, both to open the eyes of the incredulous, that if they will, they may know which is His true Faith, and embrace it for the salvation of their souls: and likewise to bear testimony to the sanctity of His servants. A multitude of such miracles, after the most rigorous examination, have been juridically proved to have been wrought by the relics of St. Dominic, St. Francis, St. Anthony of Padua, St. Edmund Archbishop of Canterbury, St. Hugh of Lincoln,

St. Richard of Chichester, St. Thomas of Hereford, St. Vincent Ferrer, St. Catherine of Siena, St. Francis Xavier, St. John Francis Regis, and a multitude of other saints.

Having now given a sufficient account from the testimony of the most illustrious writers of the Church of God, of the miracles which the Almighty has been pleased to work by the relics of His saints, for the confirmation of His faith, the manifestation of their sanctity, and the relief of those who with a lively faith solicited them to become their patrons and intercessors before the throne of God; I come now to give an account of some of the numerous miracles, said to have been performed at the tomb of the Venerable Benedict Joseph Labre, in favor of several of those, who with the like lively faith implored his intercession. The earliest account of which I find expressed in a letter dated the 23rd of April 1783, that is, only seven days after the decease of this servant of God, and which was written by the Vicar General of that branch of the Order of Franciscans called the Recollects, to the Superior of the Convent of the same order at St. Omer's, of which the following is an extract.

"Reverend Father—I think it a duty incumbent on me to acquaint you that a young man, named Benedict Joseph Labre, died at Rome on Wednesday in Holy Week, in the odor of sanctity. The miracles which he still continues to work, draw to his Tomb an infinite number of people who publish these wonders. The Blind see, the Deaf hear, the Dumb speak, the Lame walk, and the Paralytics are healed: such are the prodigies which our good God works every day by the Intercession of this holy man. I should be very glad to know whether the Father and Mother of this good man are still living."

Another letter from the same person dated the 30th of April 1783, adds—

"There has been so great a tumult in the Church of S. Mary di Monti, that they have been obliged to shut it up."

Copy of a Letter from the Abbé de Lunel directed to Mr. Labré, Rector of Erin, whom the writer thought to be still living, dated at Rome April 27th, 1783.

"Sir, I think it my duty to communicate to you the following particulars which relate to your Nephew, who died like a true Saint: as he always lived conformable to the instructions and education which he received from you. I assure you on the word of a Priest, that on Easter Sunday, while they were putting on him a kind of white Rochet adorned with red ribbons, I was surprised with something, which I know not how to express; he with his left hand supported himself in a fitting posture, and seemed to me to be just ready to speak.

I then began to think that he had only been in a trance. Everyone cried out: A Miracle! Many of the most respectable persons have assured me, that on Thursday morning, the day after his death, they saw him sweat. His Confessor has told me, and he says the same to everybody, that one day observing his Prayer-Book was in a very bad condition, he thought of giving him another, but afterwards altered his mind, for reasons known to himself. The good Penitent the next time he went to confession, said to him: 'You had a mind to give me a book, and afterwards you changed your mind; you do well: and I submit.' The Confessor, who had never mentioned it to anybody, was astonished at his words. The same thing happened to him concerning an Alms which he had a mind to bestow upon him. But afterwards, reflecting that this might inspire him with motives of gain, he changed his mind. At the next Confession, the Penitent said to him in an innocent tone: 'You had a mind to give me an Alms, and afterwards you would not.' The Confessor, quite confused, said: 'Spiritual Alms is far better.' 'That is true,' said the Penitent. And as the Confessor said it quite confused, with his hand in his pocket: 'If you have a mind—' 'No,' said the Penitent, 'never give me anything.' Towards the end of April last year, he came all in a tremble to look for his confessor, and said to him: *Oh, Father, I thought that I was dead; that they had buried me at St. Mary di Monti on the Epistle side of the* altar; that there was a great multitude of people round my wretched body, who made a great noise; and that Jesus Christ said to me: '*I GIVE YOU MY PLACE, AND I GO AWAY.*' In repeating these words, *I go away,* he burst into tears. The confessor comforted him, and told him that was impossible, but that he had not sinned by thinking so. But as the confessor was struck with this revelation, and he, in consequence of what he heard from Benedict, at that very moment formed in his own mind an imagination of what he now sees: and as, after what had passed between him and his penitent concerning the book, and the alms, which I have before mentioned, he looked upon this man as a saint: he went to three of the most respectable persons in Rome, and begged they would write down this revelation made to one of his penitents, and that they would also attest it afterwards, if occasion should so require; at the same time declaring that he himself did not know what it might mean. On Holy Saturday, when he desired me to read some papers belonging to Benedict, the contents of which he did not understand, he said to me: *This is a holy Seal; he has told me most astonishing things; but yet there is something more than this which I cannot make out.* This he told me in the presence of the Superior of the Monastery where he was, and of another religious man who assisted Benedict at his death.

On last Easter Sunday, the Superior said to us: *I have a mind to present a petition to the Cardinal-Vicar, and beg of him to transfer the Laus Perenne, or Forty Hours Prayer to some other Church, because the people come in crowds all the day long. The Princes, Prelates, and Cardinals, are so hindered by the crowds from coming during the day, that they can only come at two or three o'clock in the morning.* (This continued to be the case till the 27th of April 1783.) *All the people come in such a manner to pray to God at his Tomb, that it seems as if they disregarded Jesus Christ: I therefore desire henceforward to free my conscience in this matter.* The Confessor, the Father who assisted at his death, and I, did all that was in our power to hinder him from presenting this petition: alleging that this voluntarily poor man always went to the Churches where the Laus Perenne, or Forty

Hours prayer was held: and that this practice had contributed to the sanctification of his soul. Notwithstanding which, the Superior procured an Order from the Cardinal-Vicar to transfer the *Laws perenne* to a church just by. We were very much surprised on the Friday following, to find that the *Laws perenne* was not held at the Church of S. Mary di Monti, as it had been in former years. The Confessor, submitting to the Orders of his Superiors, when he was saying that part of the Office called *None*, and had come to those words of the Psalm: *Give me understanding according to thy word*: he publicly declares that all at once this thought struck into his mind: 'Here is the explication of Benedict's prediction. They have four days ago removed the Blessed Sacrament out of the Church; and they have transferred the *Laws perenne* to another church, to give free scope to the devotion of the people, and prevent any irreverences which otherwise might possibly happen: this is what was meant by those words of Jesus Christ, *I give you my place*. That this is the meaning of these words, appears very evident to me: and indeed the whole city is of the same opinion.' This I was informed of by the Confessor himself, who can have no interest in deceiving us; and moreover, by the precaution which he took, he has proper witnesses of the prediction. I beg you will get an exact account of the first part of this hidden life made out. Tomorrow I shall translate all his papers. I am, &c.

Abbé de Lunel.

P.S. The devotion of the Faithful appears to be greater than that which the people showed at the death of St. Philip Neri. I am informed that the superiors intend to try this devotion for some days, by ordering the church doors to be shut for eight days: that they may see whether the people will at the expiration of that time return with the same fervor. None are admitted at present but the sick. The sacristy is full of crutches and bandages."

Extract of a Letter written by a Physician at Rome, to his Sister, a Carmelite Nun at Cavaillon, dated May 1, 1783.

A poor Frenchman, named Benedict Joseph Labre, died on the 16th of last month in the house of a charitable person who had taken him in. On the following morning, they were very much surprised to find that his limbs were supple and flexible, as if he had been only asleep. The miraculous effects of his intercession have been so rapid and so numerous, that to satisfy the zeal of the people, whom a strong guard of soldiers is scarcely able to keep in good order, left the body exposed to public view for the space of four days. All this time the body preserved the flexibility and freshness of a living man. After his burial, an extraordinary concourse of people assembled from all parts of Rome and the adjacent places, which still continues, and even until this moment they visit the tomb of this blessed man, who incessantly works miracles in favor of those who with faith invoke his intercession. The dumb speak, the blind see, and those who had lost the use of their limbs walk freely and return to their own houses without any assistance, and dropsical people are cured in an instant. Last Sunday, a poor woman who had dropsy was carried in the sight of all the people and laid upon the stone which covers his tomb, when they immediately saw a great quantity of very fetid water come out of her feet, and in a moment after, she found herself perfectly cured. Broken limbs are restored, and inveterate ulcers healed in an instant. In a word, cripples procure themselves to be carried and laid on his tomb; and they return full of strength and as active as if they had never been out of order. This is a sight which is repeated every day, and of which the whole city of Rome are eyewitnesses. I cannot describe to you how much this excites their surprise and admiration. The incredulous, as well as others, melt into tears on these occasions. I myself have heard several make this acknowledgment. *I could not believe what was said concerning miracles; I have been curious, I have been to see them with my own eyes, and now I am convinced.* What a triumph is this for Religion!

No one has ever seen such things as these. There are people who, without thinking of eating, from the morning even till night, never quit the place they get possession of as soon as the Church doors are opened; in order that they may be eyewitnesses of the miracles which are performed every instant.

From the time of his death to this day, they reckon up sixty-three miracles of the first magnitude. Among the rest, there is one of a young woman of twenty-two years of age, who was born dumb, and who all at once obtained the use of her tongue; they are now teaching her the language, and she pronounces distinctly everything that they want her to say.

Extract of a Letter from the Abbé de Villiers, Gentleman to His Eminence Cardinal André Corsini, to His Friend, dated May 3rd, 1783.

I do not know whether the public papers at Paris have announced the death of a pilgrim born in Picardy, who lately died in the odor of sanctity. His name is Benedict Joseph Labre:—He lived a very mortified and penitent life; he ate no more than five or six ounces of bread per day, to which he added some peelings of lemons and oranges which he picked up on the dunghills; he drank nothing but water mixed with a little vinegar; his clothing consisted of an old greatcoat, which was the same that he wore when he left the Abbey of Sept-Fonts in the year 1770; and a cord, which served him for a girdle; he never would accept either new shoes or new stockings: he never asked alms, but he received what was freely offered to him, provided it did not exceed a half sol, or half-penny: the *Miserere* Psalm was his favorite prayer: he had no fixed habitation, but he slept in a hospitium of pilgrims to whom he distributed the few alms he received: he spent the greatest part of the day in the church in prayer, and in a kind of ecstasy: he discovered people's secret thoughts, of which his confessor is an incontestable witness: he foretold the day and hour of his death; as likewise the place where he should be buried, and several remarkable circumstances which are now verified; and which he declared to his confessor under the greatest secret; his confessor's name is Marconi.—(Then giving an account of the manner of his death as before mentioned he goes on.)—The religious of the house where he first fell down in a fit, and who are a kind of missionaries, carried his body to their house, took possession of his papers, and having learned the motive of his residing at Rome, and receiving other information concerning the regularity and holiness of his life, petitioned to have his body in their church, as being the place where he commonly prayed, which was granted to them. He was placed in a passage leading to the church where he remained exposed till Easter Sunday in the afternoon, when he was buried in a separate place by order of the Cardinal-Vicar: who took the precaution to order that the coffin in which his body, which was then flexible, was enclosed, should be sealed; they were obliged to send a guard of soldiers to guard the church, and the body of the deceased, and to keep good order. They formed a Juridical Verbal Process of all that had happened, and they put an authentic copy of it into the coffin with the body. The concourse of people continues even to this very moment. The doors of the Church, and the place where he is buried, are still guarded by soldiers. It is imagined they will begin the ordinary process concerning the virtues of the deceased, as soon as possible; that they may afterwards proceed to examine the miraculous cures which are attributed to his intercession; and of which they are now preparing the memorials.

Extract of a Letter from an English Gentleman at Rome, to his Correspondent in England; dated May 10, 1783.

We have lately lost here an extraordinary poor man: his name was Benedict Joseph Labre.—His sole patrimony was the free unsolicited charity of the well-disposed. He never asked alms, and never would take anything above a bajocco, which is little more than our half-penny. If more was offered, he invariably refused it. This was some-times rashly imputed to greediness of expectation, and impatience of disappointment; and as rashly a Surgeon once struck him with his cane for it. Having got his bajocco, he would accept nothing more that day; except it was a little broth at the door of some religious house. Here he always took the last place, and stood behind all the rest of his fraternity; and when the alms-giver called to him to come forward to receive an earlier portion, as he sometimes did out of regard to his peculiar gentleness of manners; he would excuse himself, by alleging that in case the charity could not be extended to all, he could do better without it than any of the rest. One day at the convent of the Dominicans, the broth being exhausted before Bene-dict was served, the lay-brother out of compassion to his emaciated figure, insisted upon his not going away, but remaining at the door till he should return from the kitchen, when he brought him a basin of fresh soup, such as was going to the table of the community, with a pretty large piece of fresh white bread, which he had thrown into it. Benedict took it with reluctance, though he said nothing, always carrying the silence of La Trappe about with him. But the partiality shown to him on that occasion, made such an impression on his mind, that he was never more seen at the door of that convent. It is supposed that his bajocco, when Providence sent it, was laid out in bread; and that this with his broth, and the leaves of lettuce, and the pith of bruised cabbage-stalks, gathered from the dung-hill, was his whole subsistence.

(Then, after giving an account of the manner of his death, and that, as a foretaste related in the first part of this history: he goes on.)

For some days after, the press of people was greater than ever, multitudes thronging from every part of the town, and many parts of the country; many bringing their afflicted and disabled relations, infants to children, to obtain a cure, as some of them most certainly did.—I marked and am now hearing every day from different quarters, of two persons cured immediately at Benedict's Tomb. One of the most painful lameness of above many years' continuance; the other of a total privation of speech for two years and a half.—The first is now seen walking, the second is now heard talking, without any pain, difficulty, or impediment, to the astonishment of all their friends, and of a great part of Rome, so that they are both well known. Such evidence must be irresistible to anything but the most stubborn incredulity, joined to the most consummate effrontery. And we must either admit these facts, or we must believe nothing again for the future, upon the testimony of man, or any number or credibility of men.

Neither did this conflux of people consist entirely of the lower classes; some of the first quality mingled with the crowd to visit the sepulchre of the once despised Benedict. To say nothing of so many other great names, Cardinal de Bernis went to S. Mary di Monti to inform himself on the spot of the merit of his departed countryman, and pay his respects to his memory; and before he left the Church, gave orders for the body to be enclosed in a lead coffin. Thus has God himself exalted the humble Benedict, and at the same time his Church, in one, seemingly the most contemptible of her children.

Extract of another letter from the same English gentleman, to the same correspondent, dated May 21, 1783.

The Tomb of the Venerable Benedict, which is yet unclosed, and covered only with loose boards, guarded by two soldiers, is still resorted to by an unexampled concourse of people. There is an increasing confluence of all ranks, and more coaches than ever. Great numbers of cures are currently, and credibly reported to be obtained, not only at the vault where his remains are deposited; but also in other cities of Italy, by such as have recommended themselves to his intercession.—I have no room to give the particulars of these cures, which are generally deemed miraculous; though not yet declared such by authority. And indeed I have no inclination to do it without that sanction.

Extract of the second Letter which Mr. Fontaine of the Congregation of St. Vincent de Paul wrote to the Bishop of Boulogne, dated June 4, 1783.

My Lord,

Benedict continues to make a great deal of noise every day—it is said that an innumerable multitude of miracles are wrought at his tomb. It will take a great deal of time to examine them all; but I have read several most astonishing accounts of some, which I would do myself the honor of sending to you if they did not make too great a bulk. The tomb is every day visited as it was on the first day, and with the same success. One thing which has happened, and which may be looked upon as the greatest and most estimable of all these miracles, is the conversion of an English preacher from Boston, whose curiosity having excited him narrowly to examine the proofs of many of the cures performed by the intercession of the Servant of God, is fully convinced of the reality of many of them; and in consequence of this conviction, desired to be instructed in the Catholic Faith, and last Sunday made his abjuration of the errors in which he had been educated. It is worthy of notice that this Englishman is a man of as great learning and penetration, as can be expected to be found in a man educated in error.

Copy of a Letter from the Abbé de Launel to the Bishop of Boulogne.

My Lord,

I was as incredulous with regard to what was reported concerning Benedict Joseph Labre, as St. Thomas was concerning the Resurrection of Jesus Christ. Nevertheless, three days after his death, I went out of curiosity to see him. I found him fresh, flexible, and without any sign of corruption. Providence ordained that at the sight of my band (which in this country is peculiar to French Abbés) his Confessor, the Priest who assisted him at his death, and the Superior of the Monastery where he is, should desire me to read his papers (which they did not understand) and explain them to them in Italian, which I readily undertook to do: and which has furnished me with an opportunity of being many times witness to many wonderful things, and such as are thoroughly capable of curing my incredulity. This is one of your flock, the holiness of whose life publishes the praises of his Pastor.—If no other person undertakes the work, I myself will give the public an exact abridgment of his life.—I have the honor to be, &c.

The Bishop of Boulogne

The Bishop of Boulogne, who is a prelate highly distinguished both for his great learning and eminent virtues, in consequence of such authentic proofs of the virtues and miracles of Benedict, who was born in his diocese, thought it his duty to make his people sharers in his joy; and therefore in a pastoral letter which he published, speaks of the Servant of God in these words:

For the edification of the public we now take occasion to publish the extraordinary joy which is afforded to us; by the just motives we have to believe, or at least highly to presume that the number of the blessed inhabitants of Heaven has been lately increased by one of our subjects, who in April last, died at Rome in the odor of sanctity, where by living a life very austere and hidden with Jesus Christ in God, he was able to say with St. Paul, whose glorious Tomb he frequently went to revere, "the world is crucified to me, and I to the world." Although his outward appearance was very abject, ghastly, and forbidding to the eyes of men; yet his signal piety, his profound humility, his great love of poverty, joined to his generosity to the poor to whom he distributed the unasked alms he received, had attracted the esteem, the goodwill, and the veneration of all those who know the true value of those excellent virtues; but above all his assiduous and continual prayer, which you, O you false Sages of this age, endeavor so much to decry, to undervalue, and to destroy, as if it were only the contemptible practice of persons useless to Society; but cannot be too much defended, too much praised, or too much extolled. For according to a Divine Oracle, against which the crafty reasonings of human wisdom can oppose nothing but vain and sophistical arguments, it is very prevalent in the sight of Him who is the sovereign Lord of times, of hearts, and the disposer of events.

Such is in substance the account which the Latin Eulogium gives of this venerable man: which, with the approbation of the Holy See, was put into his coffin; which Eulogium has been confirmed by a number of letters sent from the same city: two of which were directed to us by Mr. Fontaine, who having been for many years Public Professor of Divinity in our Seminary, is at present in Rome transacting the business of the Congregation of S. Vincent de Paul.

Praise and glory be forever rendered to the goodness of God, who to stem the torrent of iniquity with which the world is at present overflowed, and to provide antidotes to the venom of incredulity with which it is infected, has ordered that His supernatural signs and wonders should manifestly appear in the Capital of the Christian world: to the end that the general and lively sensation which they have produced should be more easily spread into all parts, even to the most distant regions of the world; and should moreover serve for the triumph of Religion, the confusion of impiety, the confirmation of their Faith, and the encouragement of Fervor. But let praise and glory be rendered to Him, particularly in this Diocese, which is happy in having given birth to this illustrious Penitent, happier in having him for its special Patron in Heaven; but still happier if the relation or remembrance of his heroic virtues shall contribute to make a great number of persons imitators of his assiduous prayer; and of his constant endeavors to humble himself, and shall excite them to subdue their passions, to crucify their flesh, to use resolute efforts to bring it into subjection, and to bear away by violence the Kingdom of Heaven, where he now occupies a Throne so much the more exalted, and enjoys a degree of happiness so much the more exquisite; by how much more he humbled himself when on earth, and by how much more courageously he bore about the sufferings of Jesus Christ in his body extenuated with fasts and austerities. He may now, like St. Peter of Alcantara, say: "O happy penitential austerities which have conducted me to such, and so great glory." May we not also appropriate to him those beautiful texts of the Holy Scripture, as being verified in his person? "The blessing of God maketh haste to reward the just, and in a swift hour his blessing beareth fruit."—"There is an indigent man that wanteth help, who is very weak, and full of poverty. Yet the eye of God hath looked upon him for good, and hath lifted him up from his low condition, and hath exalted his head; and many have wondered at him, and have glorified God."—"The Lord hath raised the needy from the earth, and lifted the poor from the dunghill that he may place him with the Princes of his Heavenly Court,

Given at Boulogne, July 3, 1783

Signed,

Francis Joseph, Bishop of Boulogne,

By Order of his Lordship,

Clement, Secretary.

Letter of His Eminence Cardinal de Bernis to Mr. Vincent Labre, Rector of La Pelse, Uncle of Benedict Joseph Labre.

Rome, June 9, 1783

Sir,

I have received the letter you were pleased to write to me on the 26th of May, desiring me to give you an account of the young Frenchman, known by the name of Benedict Joseph Labre, who died at Rome on the 16th of April, and whom you say is your nephew. I wish it were in my power to give you a description of what happened here at his death; but the wonders which are said to be performed every day by his intercession, and which continue to this very time, have attracted the attention of His Eminence the Cardinal Vicar, who has ordered an account of them to be carefully collected, in order to examine their authenticity and the degrees of credit which they may deserve. As your affinity with Benedict Joseph Labre has put you in a condition of being personally acquainted with him; or at least of having a sufficient and continual knowledge of everything which has been particularly remarkable in him during his life. I shall be greatly obliged to you, if you will give me a particular account of what you have been able to collect concerning him, while he remained in France; as likewise all that you know of his travels, of his desires of entering into a religious state; and of everything else relating to him, from his birth till his arrival in Italy, and even till his death. I should be still more obliged to you, if you could send me some of his letters. I beg you will not leave any means untried of procuring some of them. One at least is necessary to prove the papers that were found about him after his death to be his handwriting; that thereby we may know what he himself has written. I beg you will also give me an account of his family, their occupations, their reputation, and the rank they hold in Boulogne, where it is said they are established. I am very happy in having this opportunity of assuring you, that I am, with the most perfect esteem, yours,

Cardinal de Bernis.

Extract of another Letter from the before-mentioned English Gentleman at Rome, dated June 11, 1783.

Benedict's Miracles are now going through the fiery trial of Canonical Examination: there are no less than eighty-two upon the list; many more might be added, but none but the indubitable will ever be admitted or approved by the Inquest. On the other hand, a false modesty hinders many from speaking and giving glory to God as they ought. I myself know a person cured of a disorder, which a Surgeon of the first character positively affirmed to be incurable, though not mortal, by only once visiting the Church where his remains lay and begging his prayers. And yet this cure, and many more, if not more extraordinary, will never be subjected to discussion. On Saturday, I read the declaration of a Physician of Perugia, attesting the preternatural cure of a Nun in the Benedictine Monastery of that city, and describing many circumstances attending it, both before and after it was obtained. It was, in short, thus.

The gentlewoman had been crooked and infirm from a child, but for the two last years crippled and bed-ridden to such a degree that she could not so much as turn herself in her bed, nor move any part without dislocating some joint or other. Nothing but dissolution was now expected, and she had prepared for it, nay wished for it. At this juncture the report of Benedict's death, holiness, and miracles, reached Perugia; and soon after some of the many prints of him which are daily published in this city. The Abbess of the Monastery procured one of them, and going in some form with her Nuns to visit the Sister, told her she had brought her the beggar of Rome to cure her; as none of her Doctors could. The poor Nun laughed at first, and then answered, that she had so long and so often recommended her case to the Blessed Mother of God without any benefit to the body, that she looked upon it to be God's will she should be as she was, and that she neither expected, nor desired a miracle. The Abbess, however, held the print to her to kiss; then applied it to her head, next to her shoulder, and was going on, when the patient suddenly called out, *"I am well, I am perfectly well: reach my habit."* Being habited, she went before them without help or support to the Choir; continued some time in prayer and thanksgiving upon her knees, then heard Mass, and at last joined in singing the *Te Deum* with the Community; every one shedding abundance of tears of joy and exultation.—This is the substance of the Doctor's narrative, but divested of many remarkable circumstances and particulars by him specified, as well as technical terms by him used: he declares the cure to be in every respect a perfect one, except it be of the gibbosity and crooked-ness which grew with her from her childhood, and still remains; and he concludes by assuring us of his readiness and desire to attest the truth of everything here said upon oath, unless it be the mode of cure, which not being an eye-witness to, he can only know from testimony. In effect, the Bishop of Perugia is now instituting an inquiry into these matters, and we shall soon see the Doctor's Deposition in Form. —If his present declaration needed any further confirmation, I might add, that Mr. Fermor of this place has a sister in the same nunnery, from whom we had already learnt the same, and some more singulari-ties accompanying this stupendous transaction.

I must give you one little history more and I have done. A child of nearly four years old, three weeks ago, by an unlucky fall, cut its tongue with its teeth, in such a manner, that a large end of it, and part of one side hung out of its mouth, and seemed to hang only by a thread.

The poor mother, almost distracted, ran with it in her arms to the Hospital of Our Lady of Consolation, imagining the surgeons might be able to sew it up; but they strongly asserted it to be impossible and said they could only cut away the loose part, leaving the other to heal of itself, and that the child must remain dumb. From there, she ran to the Hospital of St. Gall and received the same answer. Then, returning home and passing by the Church of S. Maria di Monti, near which she lived, she, for the first time, bethought herself of Benedict; and rushing through the guards, called upon him aloud to assist her and her child. She left the church as precipitately as she entered it, and was no sooner within her own doors than she took up a print representing Benedict at his prayers, with it touched the extremity of the child's tongue, and replaced it in the mouth; then lulling it to sleep, which after some time she effected, and slipping the print under its cheek, she retired to grieve and to pray. After about two hours, as near as she could guess, the child awoke and called for mama and for something to eat. The mouth being inspected, the tongue was found perfectly cicatrized, exhibiting no mark of any injury it had received, excepting a seam of a livid purplish cast, running partly across it, and partly along, in the same direction with the wound before. They are near neighbors of Mr. *****; and not only that neighborhood, but a great part of Rome, is daily seeing with its own eyes, a living proof of Benedict's acceptableness to Heaven—I think Thomas and myself happy in being in Rome; but more happy still in being here at so distinguished a period.

We have just now before us a conversion which has made a great noise amongst our countrymen in this city. The convert was a Presbyterian teacher at Boston in New England, was sent over upon some errand to Doctor Franklin, and though young, has traveled over a considerable part of Europe, studying the modern languages with a view to qualify himself as a professor of the same in one of our universities. At Rome (where he has not been long) without neglecting the language of the country, he turned his thoughts to religion, studied it in books, canvassed it in conversation with the Italians, and oftener with our English and Scotch priests, and viewed it in all its practices (of which this city exhibits all its varieties) from the Pope's Chapel down to the Vault of Benedict. The consequence is that his former views are now frustrated, and he thinks no more of settling at Cambridge.—On Sunday the twenty-fifth of May, he made his profession of the Catholic faith in form.—Since that he has made a spiritual retreat of some days, and on Sunday the first instant, he made his first Communion. It is remarkable that what first (under God) made him begin to judge better of Catholics, than he had been taught or taught others to do, was the behavior of the French sailors and soldiers (not always the most exemplary) at Boston; having never before seen a Catholic to his knowledge.—He seems to be under very particular obligations to the French; for what was begun by their military, one of their mendicants has completed by the odor of his sanctity, by the lustre of his miracles (which were examined by our enquirer on the spot); and by the influence of his prayers.

Extract of a Letter from the Abbé de Lune, dated Rome, July 16, 1783.

Such things as these have never been seen at Rome even in the most holy times. The English and others cry out loudly, 'It must be acknowledged he was a good man.' With regard to his miracles, the Solicitor for the Process of his Beatification, has showed me a list of near two hundred cures of all kinds of the most inveterate and incurable disorders, that have been successively performed; and which have been well proved. Accounts of Miracles are sent from all parts: and people come from the most distant places, both to give judicial testimony of, and to return thanks for their cure.

Extract of a Letter from the Rev. Mr. Joseph Marconi to Mr. John Baptist Labre, the Father of Benedict Joseph Labre, dated Sept. 23, 1783.

Speaking of the sick person at Fabriano, whom Benedict visited and exhorted to bear their sickness with patience: he says, "This same person, having, by the advice of her Confessor, invoked the Servant of God for three days successively; she each day distinctly heard his voice, saying to her: 'It is the will of God that you should continue to endure your sickness with patience.'"

A Collection of Diverse Miraculous Cures Obtained by the Intercession of the Venerable Servant of God, Benedict Joseph Labre

Extracted from the register preserved in the Church of S. Mary di Monti: which in the whole amount to the number of one hundred and thirty-six: which have been certified till this day, July 6, 1783, without reckoning many others, which have not yet been entered into the registers, on account of their not having been yet sufficiently attested.

April 19. Angelica Cardellini, aged twenty-four years, of the Parish of S. Francis of Paula di Monti, having been to visit the corpse of the Servant of God, by his intercession was immediately healed of a languor, and almost continual fever, and of a dilated vein in her breast, which occasioned violent convulsions: and at the same time she recovered her voice, which she had lost for the space of eighteen months.

On the 20th of the same month, Angelica Raura, widow, about sixty years of age, of the Parish of S. Mark, having been brought to the tomb of the Servant of God in a chair, by the help of four porters, by his intercession recovered the use of all her limbs, of which she had

141

been deprived by two apoplectic fits, from which time she had remained unable to move herself on her bed for the space of fourteen months. She left her chair in the church as a memorial of her cure: and walked home to her own house upon her feet.

Mary Quercionnie, forty-eight years of age, daughter of Nicholas, born in the territory of Maillart, in the Marche of Ancona, in the Diocese of Fermo, was for twenty years afflicted with a scirrhous tumor of an extraordinary size on her hip, with a great flow of blood, which sometimes reduced her to such extremity, that the last sacraments were administered to her; being carried, on the 20th of April, to the Tomb of the Servant of God, she obtained a perfect cure of her scirrhous tumor; and all her other ailments ceased in a moment.

On the third of May, Joseph Bonnemain of the city of Civitavecchia, coming to the Tomb of the Servant of God, was immediately cured of a fistula in his right eye, with which he had been afflicted for the space of five years, and which deprived him of sight. He recovered his sight perfectly.

On the fifth of May, Palma Sacripantie of the City of Firmo, aged twenty years, had cancer in her breast, and a continual flux of blood, accompanied with continual pains. She was moreover agitated with the most violent convulsions, and vomited up all the nourishment she took. The last three days she was reduced to such extremity, that she could take nothing: was entirely given over by the physicians, and being almost ready to breathe out her last, she invoked the Servant of God. Then falling asleep for a moment, he appeared to her and said, *Arise, and eat.* which she immediately did with a great appetite. After this, laying down in her bed, and falling asleep again, the Servant of God appeared to her a second time, and with a distinct voice said, *Arise, thou art healed.* She then sat up, and perceived that the cancer which had consumed her was gone; and with the greatest astonishment found that she was in a state of such perfect health as she had never before enjoyed.

On the ninth of May, Madam Felicia Ruzzi, of the country of Rupitre belonging to Duke Matheo, having recourse to the Servant of

God, and having one of his pictures applied to her, was cured of a chronic complaint, with which she had been tormented for the space of eighteen years, and which had confined her to her bed for the space of a year and a half, having her body swelled in an extraordinary manner, and being full of ulcerous wounds in her mouth and throat.

On the same day, Mrs. Rosa Lebeau, wife of Mr. Lebeau, Aide Major of the Castle of S. Angelo of the Parish beyond the Bridge, having recommended herself to the servant of God, by the application of one of his pictures, was in an instant perfectly cured of a painful swelling which she had had for the space of two years in one of her knees.

On the 10th of May, Mrs. Ann Pellegrini, a nun in a monastery of the city of Perugia, aged twenty-six years, being many years afflicted with a scirrhous humor, and a continual fever, and oppressed with rickets, which jointly with the scirrhus had distorted her whole body, and made her right leg eight fingers' breadth shorter than the left; so that she could not turn in her bed without being helped by the other nuns, and at every time she was turned some joint or other was dislocated. Being reduced to this miserable condition, they had recourse to this good Servant of God, and by applying one of his pictures to her, she recovered a state of perfect health.

On the 15th of May, Dominick Fassinini, of the country called The Little-Poste, in the Manor of the Marquis of Zelloni, made a vow to God, that he would visit the Tomb of Benedict. And in consequence of this vow, setting out on his journey: at his first departure found himself delivered from a gangrenous wound which covered his whole leg, accompanied with exquisite pains, and which by the surgeons had been declared to be incurable and mortal. Scarcely had he arrived at the Tomb, but he found himself entirely cured.

On the 22nd of May, Michael Goaca, a porter of the Parish of S. Laurence at Ripette, having been brought in the arms of other porters, and laid upon the Tomb of the Servant of God, by his intercession, in a moment recovered the use of all his limbs, and likewise the use of his tongue; and returned home to his own house without any assistance.

On the twenty-third of May, Teresa Spoletta of the Parish of S. Nicholas-the-Crowned, having been blind for the space of nine years, by visiting the Tomb of the Servant of God, recovered her sight in an instant.

Sister Mary Brunne, alias Mary du Cruz, of the Convent of S. Apollonia at Rome, being greatly wasted away by a convulsive cough, accompanied with sharp pains and a low fever which she had had for the space of fourteen months, and being also unable to retain her food, having recommended herself to the Servant of God, and being touched with a part of one of his garments, was instantly cured, and at the same time freed from a languor to which she had been subject for eighteen years.

On the twenty-fourth of May, Dominica Conty, wife of Mr. Conty, a Master Mason of the City of Bauri, had been let blood in the right arm in the year 1782, by an unskilled surgeon who in the operation wounded one of the tendons; in consequence of which her arm was so swollen, and at the same time so contracted, that all the faculty had resolved to proceed to amputation, as the evil had made such progress that she could not move her joints, and her fourth finger had lost all sensation. In this condition, she had recourse to the Servant of God, and when she lay down to sleep put a little bit of his linen upon her arm. In the morning when she got up, she found that she was perfectly cured.

Maria Laurentia Spadonine, forty-seven years of age, wife of Francis Tedesguini of Civitta-Vecchia, having been overturned in a cart on the 13th of September 1782, had her left arm broken, and a wound made in the right arm which cut through one of the veins and reached to the bone. Her left arm was so maimed and useless, that she could not move either her hand or her fingers. Her right arm was likewise much maimed, though she could make some little use of it. On the 26th of May, after having prayed, and applied to her arms a small bit of the shirt of the Servant of God, she was immediately and perfectly cured.

On the twenty-seventh of May, Octavia Vergaree, a native of Viterbo, living in the Square de Morgane at Rome, aged forty-six years, having with a great deal of difficulty been carried in a coach to the Tomb of the Servant of God, was entirely cured of a condition which had confined her to her bed for eight years.

Account of a Miracle Wrought through the Intercession of the Servant of God, Benedict Joseph Labre, on a Nun of the Convent of Bollène, in the Diocese of St. Paul Trois-Châteaux: Sent by M. Eymard, Archdeacon of the Said Diocese, Dated July 4, 1783.

A Nun of the Convent of the Holy Sacrament at Bollène, a few days after her Profession, fell ill of a most extraordinary complaint. For three years and a half, which her disorders have confined her to her bed, the habitual state of her body made her subject to violent pains, colic, frequent convulsions, and faintings, so that she sometimes remained as if she were dead; as likewise to vomitings, spitting of blood, and an absolute loathing of all kinds of food. To these accumulated and continued complaints, was added a great pain in her side, which made everyone fear for her life: but God reserved her to make His goodness and His power shine at a time when miracles appear to be so necessary. After each paroxysm, this good Nun was in a most pitiful state; she frequently felt most violent pains, which she said seemed to her as if she had melted lead in her bowels. After about six weeks, her condition grew still worse: she voided her excrements by her mouth, which ordinarily happened once in two days. And they were so hard, and occasioned such violent efforts that she was almost choked, and could scarcely pull them out with her fingers. The Physician of Bolene who constantly attended her, declares he never saw any complaint like hers, and that if it could be in any case lawful to shorten any person's days in order to deliver them from their afflictions, it would have been lawful to have done it to this Nun, on account of her excessive sufferings.

The other Religious, who did everything for her which Charity could suggest, performed a Novena to implore the intercession of Benedict, for her cure, and exhorted her to recommend herself to his prayers for that purpose. She replied she did not want to be cured but only that God would give her grace to suffer with patience whatsoever He should be pleased to ordain. She persevered in these sentiments till two days before she was cured: when she began to entertain a great desire of recovering her health, that she might be able to perform the exercises prescribed by the Rule of her Order; and above all that she might visit and adore Jesus Christ in the Blessed Sacrament.

On the twenty-ninth of June, which was the last day of the Novena, this pious desire was greatly increased; and she expressed an earnest wish to have a picture of the Venerable Benedict, as she heard that some of them were in the City. She several times begged of the Nuns to procure one for her. At length, they brought her one of them. Her confidence was now greater than ever: she invoked this venerable man; and at the same time desired of the Superior that the Nuns should recommend her to God in the Vespers which they were going to say in the Choir. Behold now the wonderful work of God.

While they were saying Vespers, this Nun who had lost the use of her limbs, who could scarcely lift her head from her pillow, who had lost her sight through extreme weakness, and was almost at the point of death, (as has been attested by the Physician and the Religious of that house) all at once perceived herself well. "I am cured," said she to the Infirmarian, who every moment expected her to expire: "go and fetch my habit that I may get up." "But can you see?" said the Infirmarian. "Yes, very well," said the sick person. "And is not your stomach out of order?" "Look at it," said the sick person, "it has come to its natural state." The Infirmarian, overjoyed, ran to fetch her habit; and at her return found her sitting upright in her bed. Being clothed, she got upon her feet and tottered a little. "Courage, my dear sister," said the Infirmarian, "redouble your confidence in God"; and at the same time, she knelt down and cried out: "My God, perfect the work you have begun." Immediately after this, the sick person went out of the Infirmary to go and return thanks to God. Having come to the stairs, she did not walk, but in a manner flew down. The Infirmarian, being frightened, screamed out. All the Community, imagining that the sick person had expired, some of the Religious, and the Boarders, came immediately out of the Choir, and they met the sick Nun, who was now perfectly cured. At this instant, they were beginning Compline; and that she might not interrupt the Divine Office, she went to the upper Choir to prostrate herself before the Blessed Sacrament. When Compline was finished, she went down to the lower Choir and again prostrated herself before the Blessed Sacrament, and then before her Superior. And immediately after, all the Community, overjoyed, sang the Te Deum. I leave it to you to think what passed among these holy persons on such a marvelous occasion. After all the demonstrations of joy, they offered her some broth. "Oh!" said she, "I would rather eat for I find I have an appetite." She ate; she assisted at the Rosary with the Community, and at supper time, went to the Refectory and ate with a good appetite. After having finished her supper, at which she ate more than any of the others, she desired to relieve the reader and read with a strong voice; although before, she had lost her voice. From that time she has, every day regularly assisted at all the duties of the Community, and has always been perfectly well.

Nothing can be more false than the report which was spread of her relapse. For from the moment of her miraculous cure, she has without any interruption enjoyed a state of the most perfect health. Her voice, her sight, her flesh, her pulse, her strength were all restored at once. She has not failed, nor does she fail to observe all the Rules of the Community, being the first at every exercise, both by day and by night, as if she had never been subject to the least complaint.

The Physician of Bolène, being convinced that this cure is miraculous, intends to make his report of it to the Bishop, who waits for his testimony in order to transmit the Process to the Holy See.

Signed,

EYMARD,

Archdeacon of the Diocese of St. Paul-Trois Châteaux.

Since the publication of the French Edition of the Life of Benedict Joseph Labre, from which this is translated, the following account has been received from France, viz. that "Mary Bayard, called also Mary Raymond, fifty-one years of age, wife of Peter Delatte, Labourer of the parish of Hesdigneul, in the Diocese of Arras, had about fifteen years ago been seized with a stroke of the palsy, from which time she was not able to move her leg or thigh, but they appeared as if they were dead, and were also destitute of sensation. Nor was she able to move herself from one place to another, but only by dragging herself upon her hands and knees. And for these last five years her limbs were so contracted that she was not able to sit upon a chair; but was obliged to have a particular kind of stool made on purpose for her. This poor but virtuous woman, hoping to put an end to her affliction, formed a pious design of going to the Church of St. Sulpice de Amette, the church of the place where Benedict was born, to implore relief from God, by the intercession of His Servant. In vain did her friends represent to her, that the jolting of a carriage might put her in danger of dying on the road: for so great was her confidence in the mercy of God, and in the powerful intercession of His Servant, that she was resolved to set out for that place. In consequence of this resolution, she on the twenty-eighth of June 1784, received the Sacraments of Penance and the Eucharist, and on the same day, being accompanied by nine persons, set out from Hesdigneul to go to Amette. Being arrived at the Church Yard of Amette, she was taken down from the carriage, carried into the Church, and placed near the Baptismal Font; where she remained in the most decent posture her situation would permit. Scarce had she said a few prayers, but she perceived a violent agitation throughout her whole body, and a profuse sweat from head to foot, but principally at her knees, where she also perceived a most violent pain which made her give a sudden start. Her eyesight then failed her, and she almost fainted away: but, coming to herself in a few moments after, she all at once raised herself up on her feet and cried out, *"My God, I am cured: Let us return thanks to God; and acknowledge the kindness of His Servant."*

As she had before ordered one of her sons who accompanied her to light up some candles in honor of Benedict Joseph Labre; he returned to tell her that he had no money left to put into the plate for the poor. *"Help me,"* said she, *"and I will do it myself.* "And accordingly she went, being supported by her son. After which she walked round the Church, being assisted by her two sons, who supported her on each side holding her under the arms: and she walked quickly, taking short steps like a child who is learning to walk. After this she went to rest herself at the vicarage house, where she ate some milk-soup, and declared all the aforementioned circumstances of her cure in the presence of a great number of the inhabitants of Amette, who had assembled together in consequence of the report of this miracle; and of the persons who had come with her from Hesdigneul. She then returned to Hesdigneul in the same carriage which had conveyed her to Amette, where, being arrived, all the inhabitants were astonished at the news of her being cured. The bells were rung, and a solemn *Te Deum* was sung, to return thanks to God for so signal a favor.

The weakness which the said Mary Helena Bayard perceived after her cure was the necessary consequence of her formerly inactive state, and the poor and little nourishment which she took. For, some days after her arrival at Hesdigneul, having taken some good nourishment, with which she was supplied by some rich and pious persons of that place, and of Béthune, the said Mary Helena Bayard walked on foot, both to the church, and to Béthune, even without the help of a stick; and ever since that time has done the ordinary business of her station. She has also been visited by several physicians and surgeons who attest her cure to be complete and perfect.

This day, the twenty-fifth of August, the said Mary Helena Bayard came, accompanied by several other persons, from Hesdigneul to this place of Amette, which is nearly four leagues, in order to thank God for His mercy, and Benedict Joseph Labre for his intercession on her behalf. And after having breakfasted with me[1] with a good appetite, she rested about two hours and declared to me that she does not now perceive any remains of her former complaint; she is now going to return on foot to Hesdigneul, which we, whose names are hereunto subscribed, certify to be true. In witness whereof, we have hereunto set our hands at Amette this twenty-fifth day of August, 1784.

Signed,

Playoult. *Rector of Amette.*

Bourgeois. *Vicar of Amette.*

Duhaumeaux. *Rector of Hesdigneul.*

N.B. The Reader is desired to observe that though I have here related the accounts of those cures according as they have been sent from Rome in several letters from several different persons who are worthy of all credit: yet the relation of these facts depends only on the testimony and veracity of the private persons who sent those accounts. The Church has not yet examined and given its solemn decision and sentence concerning any one of them. They are indeed at present under examination: and the greatest care will be, as it always is, taken to investigate the authenticity of every one in particular. So that no doubt may ever after remain of the divine interposition in those which it shall pronounce to be cures truly miraculous. This will be a work of time; because several steps are necessary to be taken with each one of the cures said to have been performed: as, first, the previous existence of the complaint must be proved by the testimony of the person cured, of the physicians and others of the faculty who attended him; and of other persons who knew him while in his suffering state. 2. The cure itself, or a transition from a state of infirmity to a state of health as likewise the permanency of the cure must be proved by the testimony of the person cured, of physicians and others of the faculty, and of other persons who knew the person cured both in the state of sickness, and in a state of health. 3. It must be proved that the cure itself was not effected by the means of medicines or other ordinary applications, according to the prescriptions of physicians or surgeons. 4. It must be proved that the cure was effected not in any long tract of time, but either absolutely or almost instantaneously, in such a manner as to show the impossibility of its having been effected either by art or nature. 5. It must be proved that the instantaneous cure or sudden transition from a state of infirmity to a state of health, was effected either in consequence of an invocation of the Servant of God for that purpose, or by the application of something which had formerly belonged to him. 6. These instantaneous cures must be proved, not only by the testimony of the persons themselves who have been cured, but also by the testimony of other persons who were eyewitnesses of the mode of cure. 7. No persons will be admitted to give evidence to any of these things, but those who are of mature age, sound judgment, intelligent in their profession of physic or surgery, and of strict probity and undoubted veracity. 8. Everything that they testify must be upon oath. 9. And lastly, all these things being committed to writing and properly attested by those who are duly authorized to receive the depositions of the witnesses, must be delivered to the Advocate of the Faith to undergo a most severe scrutiny before the Congregation of Cardinals who constitute the Rota.

It is therefore evident that the examination of these miraculous cures, which are said to have been performed at the Tomb of this Servant of God and in other places, will take up a considerable time. And although they are now under examination, we have not heard that the Church has as yet pronounced its solemn sentence concerning any one of them. The only ground therefore on which they stand at present is the credit and veracity of the private, though numerous, witnesses who relate them from their own knowledge and ocular demonstration. Let us not therefore presume to forestall the judgment of the Church by publishing them as incontestable miracles; but wait for the event of the present investigation, not doubting but that God will, according to His promise, by His Holy Spirit guide His Church into all truth, and continue with it even to the end of the world.

Mirabilis Deus in Sanctis suis.

Publisher, 2023: St. Benedict Joseph Labre was beatified on May 20, 1860, by Pope Pius IX. He was canonized on December 8, 1881, by Pope Leo XIII. He is buried in the Church of Santa Maria ai Monti in Rome.

Prayers, Which Were Daily Recited by Blessed Benedict Joseph Labre.

In the Morning.

O God, the Creator of Heaven and Earth! My amiable Savior! I thank Thee for the immense love Thou hast, not only for me, but for all the world: I love Thee continually above all things; and I will love Thee this day and every instant of my life: I beseech Thee to enable me to do Thy holy will; and I will love Thee continually for all infidels and sinners and will pray all this day for them, that Thou wilt vouchsafe to enlighten them. I desire to gain all the indulgences I can, to deliver the poor souls from Purgatory; finally, have mercy on sinners and infidels; grant me, my God, Your holy love; imprint in my heart the marks of Your cruel passion: I love You, my Jesus, and I give You my heart. Amen.

Holy Virgin, preserve me this day and all the days of my life from all sin, that I may not lose the love of my God, whom I will love forever. I thank Thee, O holy Virgin! in the name of all the faithful, for the great love thou bearest them; and I thank Thee for all sinners: assist them, that they may return to their amiable God; be the refuge of all, this day and forever. Amen.

In the Evening.

O God of infinite goodness! I most humbly ask pardon with all my heart for all the offences and sins I have committed; O Lord my God! I would rather die ten thousand deaths than ever offend Thee, most sweet Jesus! I remit my poor soul into Thy divine hands; and I return Thee thanks for Thy mercies to me this day. I will love Thee always; may I now repose in the act of pure and sincere love of Thee, my God. I recommend to Thee the poor souls in purgatory; help them and enlighten all those that live in the shades of death, whether infidels or sinners. I pray to You for them; I thank You every moment, my divine Jesus, for having preserved me, that I may love You still more and more; I desire with all my heart, to rest in Your holy love and grace. Amen.

Holy Virgin, I thank You, with all my heart, for all the benefits You have procured me; I recommend to You the souls in purgatory: although I sleep, I will love You, and thank You, in the name of all infidels and sinners; help them, to the end that they may return into favor with Your divine Son: I recommend my soul to You and commit it into His divine hands. Amen.

THE END.

Notes

The Translator's Preface

1. John ix.
2. Matth. xii. 22.
3. Dodwell's Free Answer to Middleton's Free Enquiry into the Miraculous Powers of the Primitive Church. P. 45.

1. The Birth of the Servant of God; His Infancy and Education

1. Letter of M. Clement, Canon, and Secretary to the Bishop of Boulogne, dated May 24, 1783.
2. Tobias, 1, 4.
3. Agebat senem moribus, annis puer; expers lascivia puerilis, quietus et subditus mansuetudini, non impatiens magisterii, non ludorum appetens. S. Bern; in vita S. Malachiae.

2. The Same Subject Continued: The Employments of the Servant of God in His Infancy

1. Deposition of His Father and Mother.
2. Deposition of his Father and Mother.

3. His First Studies

1. Francis Joseph Forgeois was a servant of M. D'Hanotel.

4. An Account of the Youth of Benedict. His Conduct Under the Direction of His Uncle: He Makes His First Communion

1. Et ejus quidem pueritia sic erat. Porro adolescentiam simili transtulit simplicitate & puritate; nisi quod crescente aetate, crescebat simul sapientia et gratia apud Deum & homines. Nisi quod præter initiativa communia, multa singulariter faciebat, in quibus potius præibat omnes, & aliorum nemo poterat ad tam ardua sequi. S. Bern. in vita S. Malachiae.
2. S. Thomas, Opusc. de Ven. Sacr. Alt.

5. Sentiments of Esteem Which the Uncle, and the School-Fellows of the Servant of God, Entertained for Him

1. Letter of Mr. Emadon, Rector of Erin.

7. He Returns Again to His Parents, and Again Endeavors To Obtain Their Consent for Him To Go to La Trappe

1. "Sir, among the letters which I send to you, there is one from Mr. Vincent, uncle of the Venerable Benedict Joseph Labre. His testimony ought to make so much the more impression, as he is one of the most worthy priests that I know. His extraordinary piety, his austere life, his generous and compassionate charity for the poor, have gained him the esteem and veneration of the public to such a degree, that in places where he is known, he is already canonized by the voice of the people; for they commonly call him, not Mr. Vincent, but Saint Vincent," Bishop of Boulogne. Letter of June 18, 1783.

13. The Manner in Which the Servant of God Lived at Rome, After He Had Fixed His Residence in That City

1. All his movables consisted in a little basket, wherein he used to keep his Breviary and some other books of devotion, and a wooden bowl in which he received his broth at the gates of the monasteries. A piece of it is broken off at the edge, so that it could not be filled; and as it had been split through the middle, he had got it cramped with three pieces of iron wire.

16. Relates the Extraordinary Things Which Happened Either Before or Immediately After the Death of the Servant of God

1. The different places where, since the month of August last past, accounts of miraculous cures have been published, without mentioning Rome, are at Urbino, Perugia, Fermo, Macerata, Recanati, Loreto, Camerino, Cefalù, Orvieto, Ancona, Tolentino, Velletri, Rieti, Montefiascone, Monte San Savino, Narni, Civita Vecchia, Gubbio, Tolentino, Fabriano, Urbania, Montalboddo, Heltanno, Cascia, Capua, Caprarola, Nocera Umbra; in the Diocese of Nepi, Massa Lombarda, in the Diocese of Imola, Stipes; in the Dioceses of Rieti, Selci, Monte Lupone; in the Diocese of Loreto, Monterotondo, Monte Porzio; Montalto, Vetralla; in the Diocese of Viterbo, Anguillara; Diocese of Sutri, Sisterna, Dioceses of Velletri, Capo-di-Monte; Dioceses of Monte Siascone. And out of the Ecclesiastical State, at Geneva, Malta, Milan, Bergamo, Naples; and in these different states, Bari, Capua, L'Aquila, Mont Royal, Amatrice, Avezzano, Petreto, Sperlonga, Rocca di Botte, La Sainte-Marie, Capistrello, Arce, in France, Bollène, in the County of Venaissin; at many places in Artois; at Aix in Provence, Lille, Cavaillon, and many other places.
2. Eccles. xi. 12, 13.
3. , Tom. 3. P. 179.

A Collection of Diverse Miraculous Cures Obtained by the Intercession of the Venerable Servant of God, Benedict Joseph Labre

1. Playoult; Rector of Amette, and one of the Commissaries appointed by the Bishop of Boulogne to take information concerning Benedict Joseph Labre.